BOUNDARIES WERE FIRST, POWER IS SECOND

A Guide for the Empath Who's Done Surviving and Ready to Reign

by Britton Lee, MPH

Copyright © 2025 by Britton Lee Carter

All rights reserved.

No part of this book may be reproduced, stored in a retrieval system, or transmitted in any form or by any means — electronic, mechanical, photocopying, recording, or otherwise — without the prior written permission of the publisher, except for brief quotations in reviews.

This book is sold subject to the condition that it shall not, by way of trade or otherwise, be lent, resold, hired out, or otherwise circulated without the publisher's prior consent in any form of binding or cover other than that in which it is published and without a similar condition being imposed on the subsequent purchaser.

Important Notice & Disclaimer

This book is intended for educational, informational, and personal growth purposes only. It is not intended to diagnose, treat, cure, or prevent any mental health or medical condition, nor is it a substitute for professional mental health care, medical care, legal advice, or other professional services.

The topics discussed in this book include emotionally difficult experiences, including harm, abuse, mistreatment, bullying, and distressing dynamics in families, workplaces, and institutions. Readers who are experiencing emotional distress, psychological harm, trauma, or ongoing suffering are strongly encouraged to seek support from a qualified mental health professional.

Additionally, some situations described in this book may involve conduct that could have legal implications, including harassment, abuse, discrimination, or workplace and institutional misconduct. This book does not provide legal advice, and nothing in it should be construed as such. Readers are encouraged to consult a qualified attorney or legal professional regarding their specific circumstances.

The author and publisher make no representations or warranties regarding the accuracy, completeness, or applicability of the information in this book to any individual situation and disclaim any liability arising directly or indirectly from the use or application of the information contained herein.

About the Perspective of This Book

This book is largely informed by the author's lived experiences, personal observations, and professional reflections. As such, it represents one perspective among many and does not claim to offer universal, absolute, or exhaustive answers to the complex situations it discusses.

Human relationships, institutions, and personal circumstances vary widely, and no single framework or approach will apply equally to every person or every situation. Readers are encouraged to use their own judgment, discernment, and critical thinking when engaging with the ideas in this book, and to adapt what is useful while setting aside what does not fit their context.

Nothing in this book should be interpreted as definitive doctrine, rigid rules, or an authoritative prescription for how anyone must think, feel, or act.

Fictionalization & Similarity Disclaimer

The scenarios, examples, and stories contained in this book are either fictional or have been generalized and anonymized for illustrative purposes. Any resemblance to actual persons, living or dead, or to actual events is purely coincidental. No identification with actual individuals, institutions, or situations is intended or should be inferred.

ISBN:

Paperback 979-8-218-92224-5

E-book 979-8-218-93445-3

Library of Congress Control Number (LCCN): 2026903908

Printed in: USA

Published by Britton Speaks LLC, New York, NY

Cover art by Britton Lee

Boundaries Were First, Power Is Second

If we needed a reason to look up,

would stars sparkle,

moons glow and birds fly?

Britton Lee
Wonder: A New Testament

AUTHOR'S NOTE

This book grew out of my lived experience, long observation, and many years of watching people — including myself — try to stay whole in relationships, families, workplaces, and institutions that do not always make that easy. For a very long time, I struggled to understand why interactions with people and institutions would so often end with unfair social pressure placed squarely on my shoulders to bear — a kind of pressure that demanded a performance in which I had to shrink or dishonor myself.

Over time, that performance became increasingly impossible to maintain. As I aged, I found myself less able — and less willing — to continue it, which allowed me to see more clearly how the world responded to my full presence and to my refusal to perform. At first, this shift was often met with retribution and consequence in both personal and professional relationships. But over time, I learned to build new relationships from a different and more sovereign starting point, with a clearer understanding of when it was time to walk away — and whether certain relationships were ever worth beginning at all.

What you will find here is not a set of rigid rules, nor a promise of simple answers. It is a collection of perspectives, patterns, and practices that have helped me and others think more clearly about boundaries, power, and self-respect in difficult situations.

The stories and examples in these pages are meant to illuminate common dynamics, not to define anyone's life or prescribe a single "right" response. Human situations are complex, and context always matters. I hope you will take what resonates, question what doesn't, and adapt what you find here to your own circumstances and values.

Some of what this book touches on can be painful. If you are carrying deep wounds, ongoing distress, or situations that feel overwhelming or unsafe, you deserve support that goes beyond what any book can offer. I hope you will consider reaching out to a trusted professional or support system if that is the case.

My wish is simple: that these pages help you see yourself more clearly, stand a little more firmly in your own life, and move with a bit more freedom and self-trust in the places where it has been hardest to do so.

I had to learn much of this the hard way, and it is my hope that sensitive souls across the globe might be spared some of that pain by learning from my struggles and my hard-won insights.

Author's Bio: How I Got Here

I didn't come to this work through theory alone. I came to it through my own nervous system.

I am a highly sensitive person living in a world that often misunderstands, overwhelms, and quietly punishes my sensitivity. Long before I had language for any of that, I only knew that I felt too much, noticed too much, and was affected too deeply by things other people seemed able to ignore. Like many sensitive and neurodivergent people, I learned early how to adapt, how to shrink, how to become "functional" in environments that were never designed for a nervous system like mine.

Professionally, I took a different path. I earned a Master's degree in Public Health and spent my career working in clinical research and public health, learning how to think in data, systems, and patterns. For a long time, those worlds—my inner experience and my professional training— felt separate. But eventually, they began to inform each other.

At some point, I started doing what I knew how to do best: I began studying my own life the way I would study a system. I used my training in research and data analysis to make sense of my experiences, my patterns, my burnout cycles, and my relationships. And in doing so, I began to see something much larger than myself.

I started to recognize the recurring ways highly sensitive and neurodivergent people are treated—across families, schools, workplaces, relationships, and institutions. I saw the same dynamics repeat: subtle pressure to override ourselves, to tolerate too much, to explain our boundaries, to doubt our perceptions, to make ourselves easier to manage. I saw how often sensitivity is framed as a flaw, when in reality it is a powerful form of perception.

And I saw the cost.

When sensitive people are chronically overstimulated, dismissed, or forced to self-abandon in order to belong, the long-term consequences are not abstract. They show up as burnout, anxiety, depression, exhaustion, loss of self-trust, and a quiet sense of disconnection from one's own life. The more I looked, the clearer it became to me: this is not just a personal or cultural issue. It is a public health crisis—one that is still profoundly under-recognized and under-addressed.

This book is not written from the perspective of someone who has always known how to do this well. It is written from the perspective of someone who had to learn—through struggle, through missteps, through trial and error—how to build a life that didn't require constant self-abandonment.

Everything in these pages has been shaped by both lived experience and professional training. It has been informed by what I've studied, what I've observed, and what I've had to practice myself: how to understand a sensitive nervous system, how to build real boundaries, how to stop contorting myself to stay acceptable, and how to return to a sense of inner authority that doesn't depend on other people's approval.

At some point, I stopped asking, "What's wrong with me?" and started asking a much better question: "What is this system asking of people like me—and at what cost?"

That question changed everything.

I don't believe sensitivity is something to be managed or overcome. I believe it is a form of intelligence. A form of perception. And, when properly supported, a form of leadership.

The work you are about to read is not about becoming someone else. It is about becoming more fully yourself—without apology, without chronic self-betrayal, and without confusing endurance for strength.

If you are reading this, there is a good chance you already know what it feels like to survive by adapting. My hope is that this book helps you learn how to live by *self-trust* instead.

Table of Contents

Introduction: The Unseen Power Plays Empaths Endure

Even before you knew the term "empath," you were already navigating a world wired for dominance, manipulation, and control. You sensed tension in rooms others insisted were safe. You heard the subtext no one dared to name or acknowledge. You saw the micro-aggressions passed off as jokes, the dismissiveness hidden beneath smiles, the shifting energy when truth got too close.

You felt it.

Long before you had words, you were encountering power plays— subtle enough to make you second-guess yourself, yet sharp enough to leave lasting imprints on your nervous system. You thought:

"Maybe I'm too sensitive."

"Maybe I imagined that."

"Why do I always feel off around this person?"

"Why does this system exhaust me, even when I'm doing everything 'right'?"

"Why does my voice get squeaky or overly polite when I ask for what I need"

"Why do I feel guilty for wanting space?"

They said you overreacted, so you learned to quiet your responses. Then they said you didn't care, because you no longer reacted at all. That's when you realized: if you're not careful, you'll drown in a soup of contradictions—seasoned with other people's complaints and stirred by their frustrations.

What you have been experiencing is a field shaped by emotional control—where unspoken rules rewarded the loudest voice, punished dissent by labeling it as noncompliance, and discredited intuitive knowing as weakness.

These moments didn't just happen in school or work. They happened in churches, at family dinners, and in the workplace. In friend circles that policed your growth. They were woven into culture, religion, professionalism, and even activism.

The empath's nervous system often registers disruption before the conscious mind can name it. That's your power. But without context, you mistake it for your flaw.

This book is your context. This book is a reclamation.

It's NOT a guide for becoming an sensitive person. ***It's a guide for remembering and knowing the power that comes with being one.***

This book is specially meant to assist the empath and the neurodivergent who has already learned to set better boundaries AND is now ready to fully step into their power.

This book will name the common tactics others use to distort your perception.

It will validate the weight you've carried without knowing it.

It will call out the systems that siphon your energy while demanding your silence.

And it will show you how to return to your center of gravity—not by becoming someone else, but by becoming sovereign within your own body. Un-owned, un-possessed, and un-bought.

You aren't just sensitive.

You are perceptive.

You are accurate.

But in a world where accuracy threatens illusions, you were told to doubt yourself. Dismiss your knowing. Minimize your impact.

This book is a sacred refusal.

It's a manifesto for the sovereign empath—one who remembers their perception is not a liability, but a leadership trait.

A refusal to keep shrinking and an unwillingness to contort.

A refusal to keep twisting your light into shapes that make others comfortable.

A refusal to keep apologizing for what you see, what you feel, and what you carry.

Sensitive souls are too familiar with having to contort themselves to ensure their safety around volatile individuals. Many of us have learned to tap dance on eggshells just to survive. We home in on the minute shifts in a room—the way someone pauses their breath, scratches their wrist, heaviness in the air, or how the group's energy changes when a certain voice enters a room. These weren't random observations. They are part of a sacred survival skill that many people never had to learn—but you did... you had to.

Yes, it was born from trauma. From learning how to stay safe. From needing to stay ahead of danger. But don't mistake it as a flaw.

This is perception. This is pattern recognition. This is special. A powerful skill. A kind of bat sense we've developed to read a room— to detect data points others miss.

Let's call it what it is: **a scared antenna**.

A skill only cats are fluent in, and birds pray never to be noticed by.

Just because this depth of perception appears useless to the world, doesn't mean it has to be useless to you. Just because the world does not value your insight, doesn't mean it isn't valuable. And it doesn't mean you can't do something mighty with it.

They call us sensitives. The neurodivergent. Neuro-spicy. On the spectrum. But that's only because they haven't yet reclaimed words like *magical* **or** *divine*. But we don't need their recognition nor acknowledgement in order to know who we are.

We touch, sense, see and smell the world with nuance. We possess a kind of awareness that moves between worlds. The kind of knowing that senses what others haven't yet admitted to themselves.

If this sounds like you, I'm offering this book to reveal your power.

To help you stop apologizing for what you feel.

To show you how to use your wand—rather than fear what it reveals.

You were never too sensitive. You were never too much.

You've simply been powerful in a world that's afraid of what it cannot control.

This is NOT another book about healing.

It's a field guide for remembering what's already in you.

You—yes, you reading this—are NOT broken.

You are a truth-teller whose voice has been coated in self-doubt.

You are a light carrier who's been told your glow is too much.

You are a mirror who's been punished for reflecting what others refuse to face.

Let this be the text that reminds you: Your sensitivity is not a symptom. It's a signal.

Your empathy is not a wound. It is a weapon of sacred disruption.

You were never powerless.

You've always been powerful—only taught to forget it.

Welcome back.

Welcome to the remembering.

Now, let's begin...

Welcome Flamekeeper,

This is not a textbook in the traditional sense. It is a map of awakening—practical, mythic, and ancestral.

Here, we begin by helping you see the game before you try to win it. We unearth the invisible laws beneath institutions. We learn the language that silences—and the one that sets free. We study how to be present in spaces not made for you, without losing yourself.

You are not here to react. You are here to rearrange. Quietly. Deliberately. Without apology.

This guidebook will teach you how.

Chapter 1

1.1 Power as Structure, Strategy, and Illusion

Power is rarely what it appears to be. Most people chase positions, titles, or visibility—mistaking them for power. But true power often hides in silence, structure, and story.

We grow up learning to obey power that presents itself in uniforms or podiums. But the real architects of power are those who shape perception, set agendas, and create the frameworks within which everyone else must operate.

To understand power, you must become a mapper. Begin by asking:
- Who created this space?
- Whose voice is amplified?
- What emotions are allowed here?
- What happens when someone breaks the unspoken rule?

Once you begin mapping power, you realize something sacred: **power can be bent**. And it is bent <u>not</u> through confrontation, <u>but</u> through **coherence**.

When you are internally aligned, you become unpredictable to a system built on scripted behavior. **The system expects compliance or chaos**. *Coherence is something else entirely.*

To bend power, you must begin to control the rhythm of your presence. Your pauses become more potent than your performance. You start to shape the field through subtleties: posture, tone, silence, and gaze.

Power is like water—it takes the shape of the container it's in. You are that container. This section will walk you through daily reflection prompts, institutional case studies, and field awareness practices to help you trace and bend power through rhythm, tone, and sovereign embodiment.

Power Mapping Tools

To begin mapping power, consider these diagnostic questions across three levels:

1. **Personal** – What beliefs have I inherited about power? Whose approval have I sought? What do I fear losing when I speak up?

2. **Social** – Who dominates conversation in my workplace, community, or family? Who is centered in group decisions, and who is left out?

3. **Institutional** – What values are embedded in the rules or policies I encounter? What consequences are unspoken but clearly felt?

Exercise: The Power Constellation Map

List the names of the people, systems, organization, or narratives that shape your daily decisions. Consider the major characters at work, in your household, family, community and the people who have a massive "question mark" hovering over their heads. List some of the people, places and things that have had a positive impact on your life. Also consider the events in your past, present and future that are emotionally charged. Summarize them in just 1 to 3 words such as, looming bills, John's letter, talk with Pam, upcoming meeting, etc.

________________ ________________ ________________

________________ ________________ ________________

________________ ________________ ________________

Take the list from step 1 and separate them based on the predominate meaning you have attached to them using the following categories: Inspiration, Safety, Confusion, Constraint. Use the following definitions to help you determine where each item goes in the table below.

Inspiration- for the people and events that make you feel:

>   inspired

>   energized

>   hopeful

Safety- for the people and items that make <u>you feel:</u>

>   safe

>   calm

>   warm

Confusion- for people and items that cause you to feel

>   regret, hesitation

>   uncertain, doubt

>   question your value or self-worth (do I matter?)

Constraint- for the people and items that make you feel like <u>you:</u>

have few options, rejection

have limitations or barriers

must operate under pressure

Here's an example:

Inspiration	Safety	Confusion	Constraint
Grandma	Talk with Pam (neighbor)	Cousin Chuck	Parents
		John's letter	Brian (work)
			Tomorrow's meeting
Art class		Sherry's comment	

<u>Table</u>

Inspiration	Safety	Confusion	Constraint

This map isn't for blame—it's for clarity.

After completing the table, begin to ask yourself what stories or narratives come up for you. With each item listed, consider what character you may feel assigned to (victim, victor, loner, teacher, mentee, loser, immature, etc...).

The stories we tell ourselves often imply the character we think we are playing or the role that we feel has been imposed onto us by others. Stories also represent a perspective, which means all stories can be seen from new angles and perspectives as we lean into greater reflection and take on greater accountability for how we show up, take up space, respond, and how grant access to our lives and energy.

Stories of Subversive Influence

- **Harriet Tubman** moved entire networks by using songs, signals, and silence. She was "invisible" to the dominant system, yet her presence reconfigured lives.
- **James Baldwin** bent literary and social power by speaking spiritual truth within political discourse—never letting the system define the terms.
- **Indigenous matriarchs** have maintained governance through councils, circle leadership, and seasonal wisdom, even when colonial power attempted to erase their lineage.

Each of these figures shifted power not by domination, but by refusing false visibility and by radiating coherence.

Reflection Practices

The Sovereign Audit: Reflect on your week. Where did you conform when you felt the pull to resist? Where did you pause, and did that pause create a ripple in the people around you?

____

____

____

____

2. **The Echo Test**: Think of a room you often enter. When you leave, what remains? What memory of you reshapes the field?

____

____

____

Architectural Reframing: Choose a power dynamic in your life. Write a script where you reframe the interaction—where your rhythm and coherence shift the outcome.

These tools, when used regularly, reshape how you perceive and interact with the world. Power stops being something you fear—and becomes something you design with.

1.2 Language as a Weapon and a Portal

Words do not merely describe the world—they create it.

What we are allowed to name, we are allowed to transform. What remains unnamed, remains in bondage. Language forms the scaffolding of belief and the structure of our shared hallucination of reality.

Language has long been used to create social prisons. Phrases like "inner city," "collateral damage", "illegal alien", or "too woke" are not neutral descriptors. They are spells designed to distort. Designed to depersonalize.

But language can also be a portal. Metaphor, poetry, and story are tools that reach beneath resistance. The language of your soul will never sound like the language of systems. That's why it's sacred.

To reclaim language is to reclaim perception.

Sacred Alphabets and the Geometry of Sound

In many traditions, language is multidimensional:

- In **Hebrew mysticism**, each letter holds a number, a shape, and a sacred vibration.
- In **Ifá divination** from West Africa, verses are not recited—they are sung as vibratory codes.
- In **Sanskrit**, mantras are not mere affirmations—they are frequency containers that alter reality when spoken with precision.

Narrative Reframing Techniques

Narrative reframing is the art of unbinding the soul from imposed stories. Turn "I was too sensitive" into "I was wired for sacred perception." Reframe "I failed" as "I disrupted the rhythm of a system that required my disconnection."

Reframing doesn't deny truth—it reclaims authorship.

Exercises and Practices

Liberatory Lexicon – Write a list of ten phrases or descriptions you hear regularly that carry implicit violence, distortion, or reduction. Rewrite each one into language that honors humanity, spirit, or complexity.

_______________________________   _______________________________

_______________________________   _______________________________

_______________________________   _______________________________

_______________________________   _______________________________

_______________________________   _______________________________

2. **Invocation Rewrite** – Take a daily habit (checking email, going for a walk) and write a poetic invocation you speak before the action. Make it mythic. Example: "I now open the gateway of digital communion to receive only that which honors my rhythm."

3. **Mythic Voice Journaling**– Begin a journal where you write about your life not in plain fact, but in mythic metaphor. Practice saying, "There was once a child born with wind in her bones and thunder in her laugh…" and let your voice unfold from there.

When you re-enter your day with sovereign speech, systems start to lose their grip—not because you shouted them down, but because you stopped letting them name your reality. This is the start of defining your life, actions, and world in your own terms, rather than passively allowing the world to define your life.

Why Language Shapes Liberation

Most people think of language as descriptive—a mirror of what is. But in every ancient and Indigenous tradition, language is first **creative**. It shapes the invisible into the visible. It names possibility. It encodes history. It seeds futures.

Think of creation stories across cultures: the Word is spoken before the world is formed. Vibration comes before manifestation. What you say, you set into motion.

So if the language you're surrounded by is based on fear, scarcity, competition, or pathology—your nervous system, identity, and choices begin to reflect that framework. Sovereign speech breaks that cycle.

Language, Identity, and Emotional Programming

Consider how childhood language shapes identity:

- "Don't be so dramatic" = your depth is dangerous.
- "Boys don't cry" = emotions will cost you belonging.
- "You're too sensitive" = perception is a flaw, what you fee is wrong.

Over time, language like this becomes internalized—not just as thought, but as body memory.

When we reclaim our language, we begin to rewrite old programming with something aligned, liberating, and alive.

The Neuroscience of Reframing

Modern neuroscience confirms what spiritual traditions have always known: the brain responds to story more than data. Metaphor and imagery activate broader parts of the brain than literal speech.

When you change your internal narrative, you rewire your emotional response.

<u>Try this:</u>
- Replace "I'm overwhelmed" with "I'm in the fire of transformation."
- Replace "I can't do this" with "I'm gathering the strength to emerge."

These aren't affirmations meant to bypass pain. They're deeper signals to your body that ***you are not powerless inside the experience***.

Collective Language as Cultural Magic

Movements rise or fall based on the language they carry.

- "Black Lives Matter" was powerful because it declared a non-negotiable truth.
- "Me Too" worked because it was collective, not individual.
- Global Majority" reframes people of color as the world's actual majority—not the marginal few.

When language shifts, power shifts.

Exercise: The Liberation Lexicon

Create a three-column journal exercise:

Language I Inherited – Write phrases or sayings you heard growing up or in dominant spaces.

Impact on My Being – Write how those statements made you feel, act, or silence yourself.

Sovereign Rewrite – Write a new phrase that affirms truth, complexity, or healing.

For example:
- **Inherited**: "Don't talk back."
- **Impact**: I fear expressing disagreement.
- **Rewrite**: "My voice carries wisdom, even when it challenges comfort."

This is not about being poetic for poetry's sake. This is about giving your nervous system new instructions for how to be in the world.

Once you begin to speak differently—you begin to live differently.

1.3 Embodiment and Strategic Presence

Many people are disconnected from their bodies—and not by accident.

We live in systems that reward disembodiment. Systems that value output over intuition, appearance over presence, and logic over felt sense. For many, especially those who've experienced trauma, being in the body hasn't always felt safe.

So if embodiment feels foreign, or even frightening, start here:

- Begin with sensation, not control. Ask yourself: What does my stomach feel like right now? My chest? My jaw?
- Don't try to fix. ***Just notice***.
- Choose one daily moment to pause and ask: "Am I present in my body, or ahead of myself?" AND "What subtleties do I feel in body?"

Embodiment is not a performance. You don't have to be graceful or athletic. You don't need to be at peace all the time. You simply need to return.

You can begin embodiment with a single breath.

Embodied Integrity and Power

When you are embodied, your power feels less like "control" and more like "clarity."

- You don't need to dominate a room. You **settle** it.
- You don't need to speak over others. You speak ***from center.***
- You stop trying to manage perception and begin to ***hold presence***.

Even if the world doesn't fully understand you—they feel you.

That's where real impact begins.

Practice for the Hesitant Beginner

Try this gentle invitation each morning:

Place one hand on your chest, one on your belly.
2. Breathe slowly. Name one feeling or sensation you notice.
3. Say aloud: "This body is not just mine—it is me. I return, with care."

Do this daily, not for performance—but for presence.

Embodiment is not about arriving at a fixed state. It is about returning, again and again, until returning becomes your rhythm.

Presence can, at times, cause you to become more visible, but <u>not</u> all visibility is liberation. Sometimes visibility is performance. Sometimes it's a trap.

In a world that rewards curated vulnerability and punishes raw truth, you must discern: Is this space asking for your brilliance—or your spectacle?

There is a sacred art to being present without being consumed.
This is infiltration—not to conform, but to plant new seeds.

Strategic presence means regulating how much of your essence you share. In spaces built to exploit, withhold. In spaces built for resonance, reveal.

This section will guide you through embodiment practices, energetic boundaries, and rituals for discernment in visibility.

Understanding Strategic Presence

Strategic presence is not about being inauthentic—it's about being sovereign in your self-expression. In systems that surveil, performative authenticity is often rewarded more than quiet truth.

Ask yourself:

Am I sharing from a wound or from my wisdom?

 Is this space a mirror or a magnifier?

Does this audience feed my soul, or feed off it?

You don't owe everyone your story. Presence without overexposure is a form of self-preservation.

Embodiment Practices

1. **The Breath of Withholding** – During a conversation with people that have yet to establish trustworthiness, inhale deeply and imagine your essence drawing inward. Exhale without releasing it all. Let your inner truth stay anchored inside you. Share what is necessary, not what is sacred.

2. **Spine Check** – Before entering any room or digital space, sit for one full minute with your spine upright. Ask your body: "Do I feel expanded or collapsed?" Let your posture guide your boundaries.

Setting Energetic Boundaries

You have the right to remain energetically intact.

- Set internal permissions: "I will speak my truth without explaining my soul."

- Visualize your body surrounded by a gentle, porous field. Only what resonates with truth may pass through.
- When attention feels invasive, use breath to root your awareness into your lower body.

Rituals for Visibility Discernment

- **Mirror Ritual** – Before a public event, look in the mirror and ask, "Which version of me is showing up today?" Speak to that self with care. Give them instructions for protection.
- **Candle Code** – Light a candle before going into a space of visibility. Whisper your intention into the flame. Then blow it out as a symbol of your resolve.

For the Novice: Why This Matters

Many people associate being "seen" with being "safe." We are taught from a young age to raise our hands, earn gold stars, get applause, and be liked.

But in systems that exploit, hyper-visibility can quickly become a trap. You become the symbol of someone else's agenda. Your pain becomes someone else's performance.

That's why it is essential to understand **the difference between authentic visibility and strategic exposure**.

Strategic presence doesn't mean hiding your truth. It means **leading with what the moment can hold**—not what will overwhelm or extract from you.

What Novices Often Ask

- - "But don't I need to be visible to be successful?"
- To some degree, yes, but on your terms. Visibility aligned with your values nourishes you. Visibility driven by performance depletes you.
- "How do I know if a space is safe?"
- Safe doesn't mean comfortable. A safe space respects your boundaries, honors your complexity, and gives you space to choose how you show up.
- "I'm scared to withhold. Doesn't that make me fake?
- Withholding isn't the same as lying. It's sovereignty. Some people and spaces are not worthy nor capable of holding all of you.

Everyday Example

Imagine you're at work. You've just been through something deeply emotional, but your workplace doesn't support emotional honesty. A colleague asks, "How are you?"

Instead of answering from your wound, you can answer from your wisdom:

- Surface visibility: "I'm fine." (performs safety)
- Strategic presence: "I'm moving through a quiet time, thank you for asking." (protects truth without inviting exposure)

Novice Practice: Visibility Inventory

Make a list of a couple recent moments when you felt visible. Then ask yourself: Did I feel empowered or depleted after each one?

____

____

____

____

____

Write a boundary statement you can use when you want to redirect or withhold. Example: "I'm still integrating that experience and not ready to speak on it."

____

____

____

____

____

____

Remember, you don't need to "do more" to be valid. You don't need to "show more" to be true. The most powerful presence is the one that is chosen—not coerced.

Be seen because you decided it was time.

Not because the world demanded it.

Clarifying the Sacred Art of Infiltration

"There is a sacred art to being present without being consumed. This is infiltration—not to conform, but to plant new seeds."

Let's break this down.

Infiltration often carries a negative connotation—associated with spies, secrecy, or manipulation. But here, we're reclaiming the word through a spiritual and subversive lens.

To **infiltrate** means to enter a space **intentionally**, while remaining **aligned with your own truth**. You don't enter to assimilate. You enter to **activate subtle shifts from within**.

You are not hiding who you are—you are carrying it carefully.

You might shift your language, your tone, or your appearance **not to perform**, but to **preserve** the integrity of your message long enough for it to take root.

Sacred infiltration is not deception—it's discernment.

It's what wise people have always done when their truths were too radical, too nuanced, or too sacred to be immediately received.

Scenario to Consider

Infiltration in Professional Life

Imagine you work at a corporate consulting firm with a dominant culture of overwork and emotional detachment. But you are someone who values emotional intelligence, body awareness, and deep listening.

Rather than announcing these values in ways that might trigger resistance or get dismissed as "too soft," you begin to model them in your meetings.

- You speak slowly and breathe deeply during high-stress calls.
- You ask questions that rehumanize the conversation: "How is this change impacting the people on the ground?"

- You normalize check-ins: "Before we jump into numbers, let's take 30 seconds to pause and gather."

Over time, people can begin to mirror you. They feel something different around you. You didn't announce yourself as a healer. You **brought the frequency of healing into the space.**

This is sacred infiltration.

You planted seeds—quietly, strategically, spiritually.

And perhaps one day, someone in that space will feel safe enough to show up as they really are... because you did first.

Closing Reflection

Visibility without discernment is vulnerability without protection. But when you choose presence over performance—something holy happens. You begin to reshape the space around you.

This isn't about hiding. It's about choosing your rhythm.

It's about becoming the kind of presence that speaks volumes—even when silent.

1.4 The Sacredness of Subversion

Subversion is not rebellion for rebellion's sake. It is sacred design. It is the art of disrupting what harms while preserving what heals.

To subvert is to expose what no longer deserves your silence. It is the strategic refusal to participate in your own erasure.

Most systems are built to reward performance, compliance, and endurance. Subversion says: "I will no longer co-sign the rhythm that drains my spirit."

The Core of Sacred Subversion

Subversion begins quietly. It's the moment you decide to pause when the room wants you to rush. It's the moment you leave a narrative that asked you to betray your intuition. It's the whisper of, "Not this time."

It isn't about creating chaos—it's about creating clarity.

Spiritual Roots of Subversion

Subversion has always been a spiritual act for the oppressed:

- Enslaved Africans braided escape maps into cornrows and sang coded directions in spirituals.
- Indigenous peoples disguised ceremonial songs as Christian hymns to preserve cosmologies under colonization.
- Queer and trans communities turned drag, ball culture, and coded language into safe havens of expression under surveillance.

To subvert is to encode freedom into form.

Modern-Day Subversion Practices

- **Silence as Reclamation** – In a meeting, instead of reacting to ignorance, pause. Let your silence disrupt the assumption that you owe a response.
- **Refusal as Medicine** – Decline the invitation to justify your worth. Let your "no" be a sacred utterance. Allow your "uh uh" to be your last word without explanation.
- **Presence as Protest** – Show up as your whole self without shrinking. In a world that asks you to perform resilience, radiate ease.

Personal Reflection: Where Have You Conformed?

Write down one space where you often perform (i.e. around parents, work, etc...). Then ask yourself: What do I fear will happen if I stop performing? And can you identify how adopted the fear?

What part of me is still seeking survival through adaptation?

What would it feel like to let go of that performance, even briefly? Why? What behaviors and actions may change by dropping the performance

---

Daily Ritual for Subversion

At the start of the day, take a few relaxed deep breaths, then say aloud: "I refuse to betray myself today."

Touch your body in three places that often carry stress—neck, chest, stomach. Whisper: "This is mine to protect."

At the end your day, say one sentence you withheld and one truth you embodied.

Imbed rituals into your life that remind you of your sovereignty and your divinity.

Use the space below to create additional rituals for yourself that are tailored to your life and values.

____

____

____

____

____

____

Remember...

Subversion is not about being angry all the time. It's about being awake: consciously choosing your response, rather being triggered into an unconscious reaction. It's about reclaiming your rhythm inside systems designed to consume you.

You're not here to burn it all down.

You're here to remind the room that a different rhythm is possible—and to *live it*.

For the Novice: What Does Subversion Really Mean in Daily Life?

You don't need to be an activist to be subversive.

Subversion doesn't always look like protest signs or public resistance. Sometimes it looks like subtle, everyday choices:

- Speaking calmly when the room expects you to rush or erupt.

- Saying "I don't know" when the system rewards or demands certainty.
- Walking away from gossip without explaining why.

Subversion is a way of reclaiming your rhythm in a world that tries to rush, pressure, and get you to conform.

Examples of Everyday Subversion

- **At Work**: You stop using corporate jargon that drains meaning from your speech. Instead of saying, "We'll circle back," you say, "Let's talk about this with more honesty when we're grounded."
- **In Education**: A teacher allows students to sit in a moment of silence before answering questions, disrupting the urgency of performative participation.
- **In Family**: You choose not to explain your boundary for the hundredth time. You let your "no" be final.

Beginner's Guide to Subversive Awareness

Track the Pattern: Notice where you shrink, edit yourself, or laugh to soften discomfort. Write down these moments.

2. **Name the System**: Is it rooted in patriarchy? White supremacy? Capitalism? Perfectionism? Or any other system. Naming the system helps you realize it's not personal—it's structural.

3. **Design a Disruption**: Choose one small way to break the pattern. Speak more slowly. Stop apologizing for asking questions. Wear something that reflects your truth—not their comfort. This is an

opportunity to decide how you can show up and respond differently, while respecting and honoring yourself.

A Novice's First Ritual of Subversion

Before you leave your house, pause at the door. Say aloud: "Today, I will not abandon myself."

Touch your heart. Touch your throat. Touch your belly.

Then walk into the world not as someone performing—but as someone practicing. Subversion is a practice. Not all at once. But breath by breath. And that's more than enough.

For example:
- Wearing a headwrap that honors your heritage in a space that pretends to be "neutral" but is really coded as white.
- Choosing not to hide your tattoos or natural hair in a workplace where the culture of "professionalism" has meant erasure.
- Wearing colors, jewelry, or fabrics that carry ancestral or spiritual meaning, even when others won't understand them.

These are not costumes—they are signals. They remind you who you are before the world forgot to ask.

1.5 Disguise, Translation, and Tactical Shapeshifting

In some cultures, the shapeshifter is not deceptive—they are divine.

To move through multiple worlds, you must sometimes cloak your truth in digestible forms. This is not betrayal. It is wisdom.

Disguise, translation, and shapeshifting are ancient survival skills. They allow those holding complexity to navigate systems designed for simplicity and sameness.

When you speak in code, adapt your tone, or shift your language depending on who's listening, it's not inauthenticity. It's transmission. You are using the available channel to carry the signal intact.

The Cultural Power of Shapeshifting

- In Yoruba mythology, **Eshu** is the trickster deity of the crossroads. He wears a red hat on one side and a black hat on the other—each viewer swears they've seen the "whole truth."
- In Greek tradition, **Hermes** is the messenger between gods and mortals—changing form, crossing boundaries, carrying meaning between worlds.
- In Black diasporic survival, shapeshifting is how we've navigated colonization, enslavement, boardrooms, and birthing rooms. W.E.B Dubois called it "double consciousness" in 1903 in his book, *The Souls of Black Folk*.

To shapeshift with sovereignty is to encode your presence into multiple languages, without fragmenting your essence.

Translation Without Betrayal

Translation is a skill. You can speak science in the language of spirit. You can speak revolution in the cadence of poetry. You can bring softness into clinical spaces.

This is not dilution—it's multidimensional literacy.

Practical Guidance

Identify Your Masks – Make a list of the roles you play (friend, teacher, partner, leader). What parts of your truth do you suppress or amplify in each role? Why?

____

____

____

____

____

____

2. **Design a Ritual of Reconnection** – Before or after shifting roles, return to your essence. Touch your heart. Speak your full name. Light a candle. Remind yourself: "This is the unchanging core." Come up with something that resonates with you are.

____

____

____

____

____

3. **Speak in Code (with Purpose)**– Instead of saying, "This meeting is toxic," try, "There's a current in this space that's not nourishing clarity." You shift the tone, but not the truth. This is an important strategy when speaking in environments that punish and/or resist direct truth telling. Consider a past moment at work or family life where speaking in code could have been useful and write it down as practice.

____

____

____

____

Reflection for the Novice

Many new to this work fear that adapting to different settings makes them fake. But adaptation is not abandonment.

Authenticity doesn't mean sharing everything with everyone.

It means being in conscious relationship with your voice.

Some truths are meant to be whispered in safe spaces.

Some truths must travel in poetry until the room is ready for thunder.

Closing Thoughts

The world won't always be ready for your full light. But that doesn't mean you dim it.

It means you learn to carry it like flame.

Guarded.

Glowing.

And utterly intact.

In other words, sometimes you must express deep truths in subtle, symbolic, or artistic ways until your environment—or the people within it—are capable of receiving the message without defensiveness, dismissal, or retribution.

Poetry is how truth softens its edges. It allows you to say what must be said without triggering the system's resistance.

A poem can carry grief, rage, and vision in one breath—when a direct statement would be silenced, ignored, or attacked.

This is not avoidance. It is a strategy of transmission. You are not diluting the truth. You are making it travelable.

Practical Scenario: In the Workplace

You're in a team meeting. The environment is competitive, analytical, and dismissive of emotional nuance. A direct critique of leadership would be punished or misunderstood.

Instead of saying, "Leadership here is disconnected from reality," you say:

"There seems to be a growing distance between what's said in here and what's felt out there."

This opens space. It plants a seed. It invites reflection without confrontation and without singling anyone out in ways that can trigger hostility against you.

Practical Scenario: In Family

A family member continues to make passive-aggressive comments about your lifestyle, but direct confrontation would escalate tension.

Instead of saying, "You're always criticizing me," you say:

"Sometimes I feel like who I've become is sitting across from who you expected—and neither of us knows what to say."

This is poetic speech. Metaphorical. It softens defense. It makes truth breathable.

You don't have to rhyme or be metaphorical. Speaking in poetry means choosing rhythm, imagery, and emotional resonance over confrontation. It's truth wrapped in care—but still truth.

1.6 Disruption as Medicine and Design

You don't have to be loud, political, or extroverted to disrupt.

Disruption can look like a gentle redirection. It can sound like a thoughtful question. It can be as quiet as choosing to take a breath when everything around you says "rush."

In fact, many of the most powerful disrupters are those who've spent years observing from the margins.

If you've ever walked into a room and felt that something was "off," but couldn't name it—your body was already trying to disrupt the illusion.

If you've ever cried in a moment where everyone else was pretending to be strong—your tears were a disruption.

If you've ever chosen not to explain yourself to someone who refused to understand—you were already disrupting a harmful cycle.

Disruption doesn't have to be a bold act. It can be a ***true one***.

What makes it sacred is your intent: to restore truth where it has been denied.

Disruption is not about chaos. It is about care.

Sacred disruption interrupts harm by restoring attention to what has been forgotten. It does not seek to provoke for provocation's sake—it seeks to reveal what the system avoids. It brings the body back into awareness. It reintroduces the breath into urgency. It honors the sacred where performance once lived.

True disruption is precise. You are not shouting—you are unweaving.

You are rethreading the world with threads of coherence.

We'll walk through micro-disruption exercises and how to become a designer of interruptions that heal.

Why Disruption Is Difficult (and Necessary)

Most of us are trained to avoid disruption. We're taught to smooth things over, to keep the peace, to "read the room" before naming what's off. This survival skill is especially common in marginalized communities, where safety has often meant silence.

But over time, silence can become complicity.

Disruption becomes necessary when the system has normalized harm, invisibility, or disconnection. And it becomes powerful when you understand that **your body is often the first to register what's been lost.**

Learning to trust that instinct—to name what others pretend not to notice—is one of the most radical acts you can undertake.

Understanding the Role of the Nervous System

The body is often the site of suppression and the source of truth.

- Your heart rate increases when someone talks over you.
- Your stomach tightens when the conversation turns toward violence.

- Your chest collapses when the space is not safe for your voice.
- -Your teeth clinch when someone pressures you to go against your values.

Disruption begins with listening to these signals and honoring them as valid forms of intelligence

The Three Tiers of Disruption

1. **Personal Disruption** – Breaking your own internalized patterns of silence, shame, or perfectionism. Example: Choosing rest over overwork.
2. **Relational Disruption** – Redirecting conversations that rely on sarcasm, gossip, or dismissal. Example: Saying, "That doesn't sit right with me," instead of laughing along.
3. **Systemic Disruption** – Naming institutional harm or bias, even gently. Example: Asking, "Who made this decision, and who was at the table?"

Each of these forms matter. Each creates a shift in the energetic blueprint of a space.

Why Designers of Interruptions Are Needed

A designer of disruption is someone who doesn't just interrupt for the sake of release—they interrupt with direction. With rhythm. With repair in mind.

They understand that some systems are too stuck to shift from logic alone.

Sometimes the most effective change agent isn't the loudest critique—it's the ***brief silence***, the ***unexpected truth***, or the ***gentle refusal*** to play along.

Closing Invitation

Ask yourself today:

- Where do I feel a subtle urge to interrupt what harms me?
- Where do I already disrupt—but fear it isn't enough?
- What might shift if I treated disruption not as confrontation—but as a sacred act?

Disruption is not detour. It's the map back to coherence.

1.7 Embodiment and World Impact

Your body is not a container. It is a field.

Your presence is your politics. Your energy is your strategy.

The more coherent you become—mind, body, soul, and speech—the more the world around you begins to adjust. Not because you force it, but because coherence exerts its own gravity.

You've already seen this: how a calm presence can settle a room. How a joyful person can light a space. How someone grounded in purpose rarely needs to raise their voice to be heard.

Embodiment Is Not Just a Concept—It's a Practice

To embody means to bring the abstract into the physical. It means your beliefs aren't just thoughts—they're actions. They show up in how you walk, breathe, speak, and respond.

You don't need to be perfect. You need to be consistent.

When your body tells the same story your words do—you become a field. People feel it, even if they can't name it.

The Science Behind Embodied Presence

Research in neuroscience, somatics, and trauma recovery has shown that:
- The nervous system co-regulates with others in proximity.
- Emotional states transmit through tone, micro-expression, and posture.
- People often trust what your body conveys more than what you say.

This is why "performing confidence" doesn't always work. But being grounded—through breath, clarity, and alignment—does.

Practices to Anchor Embodied Presence

Centering Breath: Three deep breaths. Inhale through the nose. Exhale with sound. Let your exhale be longer than your inhale. Do this before speaking in any space you want to influence.

Voice Check: Record yourself speaking about something you care about. Listen NOT to your words—but to your rhythm. Are you rushing? Shrinking? Let your voice stretch. Let it land.

Walking Practice: Walk through a familiar space slowly. Not to arrive—but to emanate. Feel the way your feet meet the earth. Let each step say, "I belong here."

For the Novice: What Is Coherence?

Coherence doesn't mean having it all together. It means having your parts aligned. It means you're not hiding your truth in one place while performing it in another.

You feel one thing, say another, and your body does a third? That's fragmentation.

But when you feel, speak, and move from the same place—you become coherent.

And coherence is magnetic. Coherence is alignment with self.

Closing Reflection

Ask yourself:

- Where in my life am I still performing safety?

- What parts of me are asking to be brought back into alignment? (think about when and where you may be performing that you're fine or happy)

- What kind of presence do I want to become known for?

Embodiment is how you stop just talking about truth—and start walking it.

It's how you stop chasing impact—and start becoming the field that reshapes what enters it.

Becoming the Field

You've just journeyed through the seven foundational principles of strategic sovereignty. This is the groundwork—not just for changing the world, but for reclaiming your deepest alignment within it.

Let's recall what you've gathered:

You mapped power, not as a fixed force, but as a malleable current you can shape.

You reclaimed language as a portal to presence and truth.

You discerned between visibility that depletes and presence that nourishes.

You explored subversion not as defiance, but as design.

You honored shape-shifting as wisdom, not weakness.

You practiced disruption as a sacred architecture of care.

You rooted embodiment as your most truthful form of leadership.

Each of these teachings is more than theory. They are invitations—into rhythm, coherence, sovereignty, and soul.

You are not here to perform. You are here to pattern. Let the world feel the shape of your being—not as rebellion, but as remembrance.

A Word of Encouragement

You may not feel ready. You may still be healing. You may still be doubting your voice, your rhythm, your impact.

But let this be known:

Every time you pause instead of perform, you shift a centuries-old pattern. Every time you speak without betraying your rhythm, you awaken new memory in the room.

You are not behind. You are not late. You are in spiral time. And every part of you is right on time.

You don't need to become someone else to matter. You only need to become more of who you already are. The unsuppressed you. The you that has learned to respond in rather than react to the world around you.

I'll walk with you.

The next chapter builds on this foundation—and takes us deeper into the codex of frequency. But for now, breathe... And breathe again... Slower... Deeper.

You've done something brave by arriving here.

Welcome to your field.

Chapter 2

The Codex of Frequency

2.1 Reality as Frequency, Not Form

You are not merely living in a world of physical objects—you are moving through a constant stream of invisible information. Every place you go, every person you encounter, and every moment you experience carries an energetic texture. This texture is what we're calling "frequency."

Think of frequency as the emotional or energetic climate of a space or interaction. Just like a room can feel warm or cold in temperature, it can also feel light, heavy, welcoming, tense, chaotic, or calm. That "feeling" is more than just a mood—it's a signal that your body is picking up on, whether or not your mind has words for it.

When we say the world is made of frequencies, we mean that underneath the surface of things—beneath the roles, the conversations, and the visible structures—there are patterns of vibration that shape how we relate, behave, and respond. These patterns are often subtle and hard to name, but they have real power.

You are not just reacting to this field—you are contributing to it. Every thought, breath, and emotional tone you carry is also sending out its own signal. This isn't metaphorical—it's biological, emotional, and spiritual. You are an emitter and a receiver at the same time.

The novice mistake is to think reality is determined only by what is visible or measurable. But as your awareness sharpens, you begin to see that what shapes experience the most is often invisible: tone, rhythm, presence, and intention. Perception is a mirror. Frequency is the sculptor.

<u>Why This Matters</u>

Every room you enter, every conversation you join, every digital space you scroll—has a tone. A frequency. A hum. Some elevate you. Some deplete you. Your task is not to analyze them endlessly. Your task is to learn to feel them. And eventually—shape them.

Most people only ever react to frequency. But the sovereign learns to generate it.

Educational Insight

In both spiritual traditions and contemporary science, there is consensus that reality is vibrational in nature.

Quantum physics reveals that all matter is energy vibrating at specific frequencies.

Biofield research shows that the human body emits an electromagnetic field that shifts with thought and emotion.

Mystical traditions describe auras, resonance, and prana—subtle currents that affect well-being and perception.

You are not outside of these fields. You are in them—and made of them.

Practice: Frequency Tracking

Spend a day tuning your awareness to frequency (aka mood), not appearance.

When you enter a space, pause. Ask: What does the room feel like? Is it warm, brittle, chaotic, dull, expansive?

When speaking with someone, notice how your body responds. Do you feel tight or open, lifted or drained?

Keep a "Frequency Log" for 3 days. Track the felt-sense of each environment you enter and note how your presence shifted within them.

The goal is not judgment. It's attunement. It's about recognizing more consciously what you dread, sense, and feel.

For the Novice: What Does It Mean to Feel Frequency?

If you're not used to feeling subtle energy, start small. It might show up as:

A sensation in your chest, gut, or skin when you meet someone new. The urge to leave a place without knowing why.

Feeling unusually heavy, tired, or overstimulated after scrolling on social media.

Frequency is not always loud. Sometimes, it's just the whisper in your bones saying, "This space is not truth-aligned."

The more you listen, the clearer it gets.

What It Means to Be a Frequency-Shaper

To be a frequency-shaper means you are no longer only reacting to the emotional climate around you—you are generating and influencing it.

Most people pass through life as receivers. They absorb the energy of a room, mirror others' moods, and adjust themselves to fit the dominant tone—even when it costs them peace or clarity. A type of self-abandonment best described as emotional contortion that can lead to stress and depression.

But frequency-shapers move with a different awareness. They know that their emotional tone, thoughts, body language, and breath are all transmitters. When shaped with intention, these transmissions change the atmosphere. It's why many African Americans can express an entire thought or idea to one another, with just a subtle facial expression that is immediately understood, although no words were spoken.

You've likely already experienced this.

A calm person enters a chaotic meeting and everyone starts to settle.

A friend's laughter in a tense moment suddenly lightens the mood for everyone.

A teacher's quiet confidence sets a tone of respect before they even speak.

This isn't about controlling others—it's about holding a steady internal signal that gives others permission to attune to something deeper and more grounded.

Examples of Deliberate Frequency-Shaping

At Work: Instead of matching the stress in a high-pressure meeting, you slow your pace, breathe intentionally, and choose words that invite clarity rather than urgency. You become an anchor of calm, even if others aren't.

In Public Spaces: You walk into a crowded train car. The energy is anxious and rushed. You close your eyes, exhale fully, and ground your feet. You soften your shoulders. You hold ease in your posture. In some occasions, others will begin to mirror that state.

In Conversation: A friend is venting and spiraling. Instead of offering solutions right away, you sit with full presence. You reflect what you're hearing with calm and compassion. Your steadiness helps them find their own.

Start Here: Beginner Practices for Frequency-Shaping

- Begin each day by choosing a tone. "Today, I carry clarity." "Today, I embody stillness." Let your breath, body, and voice express that intention throughout the day.
- In every interaction, ask: "What tone is being set here, and what am I contributing to it?"
- Notice what tone you leave behind. After you exit a space, reflect: "What lingered?"

Being a frequency-shaper doesn't mean you're always calm or perfect. It means you are in conscious relationship with your energetic field.

You don't just feel the room. **You shape it**.

When Others Can't Match Your Frequency

Holding a steady internal signal is a powerful form of leadership—but not everyone will be ready or able to meet you there.

Sometimes, your calm will irritate someone who relies on chaos to feel in control.

Sometimes, your clarity will provoke those who benefit from confusion.

Sometimes, your grounded presence will mirror someone's disconnection—and that can make them uncomfortable.

This doesn't mean you're doing something wrong. It means your frequency is creating contrast—and contrast reveals dissonance.

What It Looks Like When Someone Can't Meet You

- They escalate emotionally when you stay grounded.
- They dismiss your presence or attempt to provoke you into reaction.
- They minimize your clarity with sarcasm, blame, or withdrawal.

This is a test of your own alignment. Will you lower your signal to match their state—or hold your center with compassion and boundaries?

Responses That Can <u>Dishonor</u> Your Signal

- Overexplaining yourself to soothe their discomfort.
- Absorbing their emotional state to avoid conflict.
- Shifting your energy to prove you're "not a threat."
- Becoming reactive in an attempt to protect your truth.

These are self-abandoning patterns—ways we disown our coherence to preserve false harmony.

Responses That <u>Honor</u> Your Signal

- Taking a breath and naming the energy clearly: "I can sense this isn't landing well. Let's pause."
- Holding silence instead of rushing to fill the discomfort. That is to say, learn to become comfortable with "awkward silences".
- Saying calmly, "I'm going to stay with what I know is true, even if we see this differently."
- Choosing to disengage when alignment is not possible: "This feels like a conversation we should return to when we're more grounded."

The key is to stay in integrity without making others wrong. You're not here to force anyone into resonance—<u>they must choose it</u>.

But you are allowed to **protect your field**.

That is what sovereignty looks like in practice.

Detecting Narcissism and Emotional Immaturity Through Frequency

Your ability to hold a steady, authentic signal can become a powerful diagnostic tool—especially in romantic relationships.

When you consistently lead with presence, clarity, and coherence, emotionally immature or narcissistic individuals may interpret this as a threat.

Why? Because:

- Your calm cannot be controlled.
- Your clarity cannot be manipulated.
- Your consistency exposes their instability.

In healthy relationships, your grounded signal invites connection, reflection, and intimacy.

In emotionally immature relationships, your signal may trigger one of the following:

Invalidation: Your needs or feelings are dismissed as "too much" or "overreacting."

Distortion: Your words are twisted to create doubt or confusion.

Projection: They accuse you of what they are actually feeling—calling you "controlling," "dramatic," or "distant."

Energetic Sabotage: They create chaos when you are grounded, just to destabilize the connection, thus leaving you confused if you don't stay centered and grounded. This kind of person often shows annoyance when you're in a state of ease or relaxation.

These patterns are not always overt. But if you leave interactions feeling drained, silenced, or like you're constantly justifying your basic truth—***that's a signal***.

Frequency Can't Be Faked

Words can lie. Presence can't. When your inner signal is strong, it becomes easier to detect relationships where harmony is **only** possible if you abandon your frequency.

In romantic partnerships, that is often the first clue: when your most coherent self is not welcomed, but ***reshaped*** or ***resisted***. These clues show up as pressure to shrink yourself, over-explain, and/or contort yourself in order to stay in relationship.

The more fluent you become in energetic awareness, the less time you'll spend explaining your intuition.

You'll simply trust what your nervous system already knows.

Closing Reflection

Reality is not just what you touch—it's what touches you. You have always been a frequency-shaper. You just forgot you were tuning the signal. Now, you remember.

2.2 The Science and Spirituality of Signal

You are always broadcasting.

Even when you're silent, even when you're smiling, even when you've said "I'm fine"—your body, your tone, and your field are transmitting more than your words ever could.

This is your signal—your energetic output, the tone of your truth, the frequency your presence communicates to others.

Signal is not a metaphor—it's biology and beyond.

Modern science has finally begun to validate what ancient mystics, healers, and empaths have always known: your inner state speaks before you do.

The HeartMath Institute has shown that the human heart generates an electromagnetic field that extends 3–5 feet beyond the body.

Polyvagal theory explains that the nervous system continuously scans for safety or danger—not through logic, but through tone of voice, facial cues, posture, and breath.

Quantum biology points to the body's ability to communicate internally through bio-photons—literal light emissions from cells.

You are an electric, magnetic, and resonant being. You don't just walk into a room. You arrive.

Spiritual Traditions Speak the Same Truth

In Sufi mysticism, it is said that "the state of your heart reaches the other before your voice does."

In Buddhism, right speech begins with right presence—a cultivated inner stillness that shapes communication.

In Ifá, which originated with the Yoruba people of West Africa, a person's aṣe (vital force) is known to alter the energetic tone of any space they enter.

Your signal is not just a reflection of mood—it is the living language of your consciousness.

Understanding Signal Integrity

When your thoughts, emotions, and body are congruent—your signal becomes clear, consistent, and trustworthy.

When they are fragmented—when you smile while suppressing grief, or speak peace while holding resentment—your signal becomes incoherent. Others may not consciously detect the misalignment, but they will feel it.

Signal integrity is not about perfection. It's about honesty. About coherence. About owning what you carry.

Practice exercises: Noticing Your Signal

1. **Posture Scan:** What is your body saying right now? Is it braced or relaxed? Forward or withdrawn? Write it down below... This is what your body is broadcasting and speaking to the world.

2. **Voice Replay:** Record a voice note when you're happy, frustrated, overwhelmed or vulnerable. Listen back—not to your words, but your tone. What is really being said? Detail the nuances in your voice and tone below.

____

____

____

____

____

____

3. **Mirror Inquiry:** Stand before a mirror and ask, "What am I broadcasting right now?" Say nothing. Just look and listen inwardly. Detail the moods, emotions, and themes that are swirling around inside you.

____

____

____

____

____

For the Novice: How to Strengthen Your Signal

Speak less, but with intention. Let your words match your breath.

When you feel dysregulated, pause before engaging and resist the need to rush your response. Centering is part of communication.

Begin journaling what your body felt before each meaningful interaction. Track patterns over time.

You are already broadcasting. The question is—are you broadcasting what's real?

Remember...

The most trusted people are not those who are always "positive"— but those whose signal is authentic.

Your signal doesn't need to be impressive. It needs to be true.

And when your signal is true, your presence becomes medicine.

2.3 Tuning Your Instrument

Your body is an instrument. Not a tool to control. Not a vessel to escape. But a living instrument of frequency.

It broadcasts. It receives. It resonates. And just like any instrument, it can be out of tune.

When your body is braced with anxiety, your signal sharpens into urgency. When you're tired or disconnected, your signal gets muffled. When you're in alignment—present, rested, breathing fully—your signal becomes clear, resonant, magnetic.

Why This Matters:

If you want your presence to land with precision and grace, you must know how to tune yourself.

You can't expect clarity from a body filled with static.

Tuning your instrument doesn't mean perfection—it means preparation. It means care. It means understanding that your nervous system is part of your message.

Tuning Techniques: Practices to Realign Your Signal

1. **Breath as Tuner**

The breath is your first tuning fork.

Try the 4-7-8 method: Inhale for 4 counts, hold for 7, exhale for 8. Repeat 3–5 times to soften internal noise and slow your signal. This has a calming to your system.

2. **Sound as Resonance**

Humming, chanting, or toning your voice helps regulate the vagus nerve and recalibrate your vibrational field.

Even a simple hum or whispered affirmation can attune your body's rhythm to your intent.

3. Movement as Reset

A brisk walk. A sway. A dance. Movement reorganizes static. Don't aim to look graceful. Aim to shake loose what doesn't belong.

4. Stillness as Clarity

Sit in silence for 60 seconds before a difficult conversation. Relax your shoulders, breathe easily, and let your presence gather. Allow your message take form before it reaches your mouth.

For the Novice: What It Feels Like to Be Tuned

- You feel calm but not shut down.
- Your breath is present, and you're not rushing your words.
- You aren't rehearsing your next line—you're listening, responding, being.
- You don't feel the need to over-explain or convince.
- Your body is not bracing. You are inhabiting yourself.

Self-Check: Signs You May Be Out of Tune

- Your thoughts are louder than your breath.
- You feel "ahead of yourself" or dissociated from your body.
- Your tone is sharper or flatter than you intend.
- You're reactive, even when trying to be composed.

Remember...

You don't need to be "on"—you need to be attuned.

You are the instrument. And when you're tuned, the message will carry itself.

2.4 Coherence as Power

Power isn't just about presence. It's about pattern.

Coherence is what happens when your inner world is aligned—when your thoughts, words, body, and actions are in agreement.

You've met people like this before: they don't speak often, but when they do, everyone listens. They don't command attention—they channel it. That's coherence. It doesn't beg for impact. It radiates it.

By pattern, we mean the repeated alignment of your inner and outer worlds—the way your choices, responses, posture, voice, and values consistently express a single thread of truth.

Power is not a moment of impact. It is the trust you build when your signal is stable.

It's not how loud you speak. It's how clearly your frequency repeats over time.

True power isn't performed—it's patterned. It's the invisible rhythm that others begin to recognize and rely on, even when they don't understand why.

What Is Coherence, Really?

Think of coherence like a musical chord: when all notes are in tune, the sound is rich, harmonious, and powerful. When one note is off, the whole experience feels jarring—even if you can't explain why.

The human equivalent of **incoherence**?
- Your voice saying "yes" while your gut says "no."
- Smiling while feeling deeply unsafe.
- Agreeing to perform when your soul longs to rest.

Incoherence drains energy. Coherence focuses it.

Why Coherence Creates Influence

Coherent people don't just "say" things—they transmit them. Their message isn't just linguistic—it's vibrational.

When you are coherent:
- People feel safer around you.
- Your boundaries become clearer—even unspoken ones.
- Your presence feels trustworthy, even if people can't explain why.

Building Your Coherence: Micro-Practices

1. **Alignment Check-In**
Before any important meeting or interaction, ask: "Is what I'm about to say aligned with what I believe and feel?"

If not, adjust. Not to manipulate—but to be honest with yourself.

2. **Posture and Truth**
Notice how your body reacts when you speak from your truth, versus when you appease. One will feel upright, even if your voice quivers. The other will collapse, while making feel small.

3. **Micro-Corrections**
If you catch yourself being incoherent—pause, reset, and restate. Model repair without shame.

For the Novice: How to Tell When You're Coherent

- Your voice feels grounded and steady—not forced.
- You don't have a lingering feeling of "Why did I say that?"
- You feel more energized after sharing, not depleted.
- You walk away from interactions with a sense of dignity, even if they were difficult.

Coherence doesn't mean everyone agrees with you. **It means you didn't abandon yourself to be understood.**

Remember...

Incoherence can get applause. Coherence creates change. One chases validation. The other shapes the field.

Let your inner alignment be your revolution.

2.5 The Field You Create

You are not just entering environments—you are generating them.

Your presence is not passive. It has shape. It has texture. It holds memory.

You are a field. And that field is part of what other people feel, even before a word is spoken.

What is a Field?

A field is the energetic atmosphere around you—a space shaped by your breath, your body, your beliefs, and your emotional tone. It's the sum of your coherence, your silence, your longings, your healing.

Fields are not mystical abstractions. They are felt realities.

- You've walked into rooms that felt thick with tension.
- You've met people whose very presence softened your body.
- You've experienced how one person's calm can slow a whole group's pace.

That's the field.

Why This Matters

Most people live in reaction to fields that they don't realize they're swimming in. But when you become intentional about the field you carry, you stop being reactive and start being relational.

You become the one who sets the tone—through resonance, **not** dominance.

How to Cultivate a Field of Integrity

1. Begin the Day by Asking:
"What field do I want to bring with me today?"
Choose one word: spaciousness, clarity, trust, ease, honesty...

2. Return to It Often:
Before meetings, during transitions, after triggers—pause and re-anchor.
Breathe. Recall your word. Let your body catch up to your intent.

3. Post-Interaction Reflection:
Ask yourself: "What lingered after I left the room? What tone did I leave behind?"
This is how you become fluent in the art of atmosphere.

Important Note: It's not about being perfect, you may deviate from your day's intention. This is a practice to help you stay centered more often and with less deviation over time. Please be easy on yourself. If you feel you are off-center, take a moment to reset and recenter.

For the Novice:

How to Tell You're Affecting the Field

- People exhale more deeply when you arrive.
- The pace of conversation slows around you.
- You notice others beginning to mirror your energy, posture, or emotional tone.
- Conflict softens—not because you "fixed" anything, but because you stayed coherent.

Your field doesn't need to be big. It needs to be true.

Remember...

You are the architect of your own energetic architecture.

The more intentional you become, the more your presence becomes a place—one people remember, one people return to, even when they don't know why.

Let your field be a sanctuary.

2.6 Becoming Resonant Infrastructure

The highest form of leadership is not control. It's resonance.

You don't have to dominate a space to change it. You only have to resonate more clearly than the distortion around you.

When your frequency is coherent and consistent over time, it becomes infrastructure—a reliable pattern that others can anchor to, align with, and organize around.

What Does Resonant Infrastructure Look Like?

- A teacher whose calm centers an entire classroom.
- A friend whose honesty invites others to drop their masks.
- A team member whose grounded presence keeps the group from spiraling.
- A speaker whose integrity shifts the tone of a whole conversation online.

This isn't charisma. It's relational gravity.

You become a stabilizing signal in a world of static.

Why This Matters

Systems often organize around the most dominant frequency—whether it's fear, control, compassion, or coherence.

If you don't bring a deliberate signal, you'll get swept up in someone else's. Coherence positions you as a rooted tree that weathers storms, rather than a leaf that blows in the wind and gets trampled on.

By becoming resonant infrastructure, you don't just influence people—you help reorganize the space itself.

Practices to Build Resonant Infrastructure

1. Choose Signal Over Reaction
Ask yourself: "Do I want to match the noise—or become the rhythm?" Hold your pace. Set your tone. Let others sync to your clarity.

2. Be Predictable in Truth
Let your integrity be dependable. Show up as someone whose values don't fluctuate with praise or pressure.

3. Stabilize, Then Influence
Before trying to shift a room, stabilize yourself. When your internal signal is steady, external shifts follow more easily.

For the Novice: You Don't Have to Be the Loudest

Infrastructure doesn't announce itself. It supports.

You don't have to be a leader in title. You lead when people begin to lean into your signal for safety, inspiration, or recalibration.

If people breathe easier around you, you're already building something.

Remember...

Resonance becomes architecture when it's consistent. And architecture outlasts noise. Let your signal become the scaffolding of a new reality.

2.7 Your Signal Is Your Legacy

What you leave behind is not just your work. It's your signal.

The way you made people feel.
The atmosphere you carried into the room.
The inner alignment you held when no one was watching.

These are not minor things. They are resonant echoes—frequencies that ripple beyond you.

What Lasts Beyond the Moment?

- A parent's nervous system shapes the safety their child will feel for a lifetime.
- A healer's grounded presence can stay with someone long after the session ends.
- A creator's coherence becomes a map for others long after their words fade.

Legacy is not performance. It is patterned presence.

Why This Matters

We live in a culture obsessed with impact as visibility. But some of the most powerful imprints are invisible.

Your signal becomes legacy when it endures—when it becomes something people return to in their own time of dissonance.

It's not the applause that proves you mattered. It's the stillness that remains after you've left.

Live as a Legacy Now

1. Hold Integrity in Small Moments
The way you pause before reacting. The way you breathe in conflict. The way you exit a space with care. These moments leave more behind than you think.

2. Prioritize Resonance Over Recognition
What if your work wasn't always seen, but always felt? Would that be enough? Could that be sacred?

3. **Let Your Body Be the Archive**

When you live in alignment, your body becomes the record of your deepest truths. And others can sense it.

For the Novice: You're Already Leaving Traces

The tone in your voice and the pace of your words during difficulty.

The presence you bring when no one is watching.

The way someone feels after interacting with you.

This is not pressure. This is power.

You don't need a platform to have a legacy. You just need a frequency worth remembering.

Remember...

Legacy is not what you build on the outside.

It's what you tend to on the inside—until it begins to shape the world without needing permission.

Your signal is your signature.

Let it be unmistakable.

Chapter 3

Visibility, Infiltration, and Presence

3.1 Understanding Visibility

Visibility is often mistaken for success.

We're told to "put ourselves out there," to "be seen," to chase exposure as if it guarantees belonging or impact. But exposure is not the same as influence. And being watched is not the same as being safe.

In fact, for many—especially those who are spiritually sensitive, culturally marginalized, or narratively subversive—visibility can become its own form of violence.

To be visible in a space that has not yet made room for your full truth is to risk misinterpretation, tokenization, or attack.

That's why **strategic presence** matters more than exposure.

Educational Insight: The Performance of Visibility

In modern systems of power, visibility is often rewarded when it is non-threatening—when it affirms the status quo, entertains without confronting, or reveals without destabilizing.

But visibility that carries truth is often punished. Why?

Because most modern systems are designed to metabolize performance—not presence.

To remain whole while being seen requires discernment. To show up without diluting yourself is an act of precision.

For individuals whose bodies, clothing, or identities already fall outside the norms of dominant culture—such as those who are gender nonconforming or racially marginalized—part of their truth is often exposed by default. The visibility of their difference can precede any spoken word. In these cases, strategic presence is not about hiding—it's about choosing *how* and *when* to engage deeper layers of self.

You can't control how others perceive your appearance, but you can control the energetic boundaries you set, the timing of your revelations, and the frequency you hold. Strategic presence in this context becomes a way of protecting your essence while still being real.

You do not owe full emotional transparency to a world that hasn't earned your trust.

Practice: Track Your Visibility Triggers

Begin by noticing:
- Where do you feel the urge to be seen? (think places and circumstances)

- When do you feel overexposed after showing up?

- What spaces reward performance, but not presence?

Journal these observations. Over time, patterns will emerge—patterns that teach you where your truth thrives, and where it is siphoned.

Infiltration

Infiltration is not deception. It is sacred strategy.

To infiltrate means to enter a space not to conform, but to shift the center of gravity from within. It means withholding your full essence until the space can metabolize your presence.

Infiltration allows you to remain intact while engaging environments that are not yet ready for your full frequency

You may not change the system all at once, but your coherence acts like a tuning fork—inviting others to harmonize not because you demanded it, but because they sensed a truer rhythm and chose to attune.

Workplace Scenario

An empath enters a corporate meeting where urgency and performative productivity dominate the energy. Though others speak rapidly, compete for airtime, and avoid vulnerability, the empath chooses to speak slowly, asking clarifying questions and naming what's emotionally present in the room. Instead of mirroring the rush, they ground their presence and make space for reflection. Over time, others may begin to slow down when they speak, feeling safer in the calm the empath consistently brings.

Social Interaction Scenario

An emotionally immature friend launches into a story rooted in blame and victimhood. The empath feels pressure to nod, validate, and go along with the narrative. Instead, they pause, breathe, and stay grounded. When the friend finishes venting, the empath gently says, *"It sounds like that really hurt you. Is there something you were needing that you didn't get in that moment?"* This statement and question shift the focus from blame to need, and from projection to reflection. Their voice is calm, their posture open. The friend may not acknowledge the shift in the moment, but the empath's energy begins to de-escalate the emotional charge, inviting honesty without shame. Without confrontation, the empath redirected the interaction toward honesty and self-awareness—shifting the relational dynamic without force.

Family Scenario

A controlling parent attempts to dominate a conversation with their adult child, using guilt and subtle emotional manipulation to reassert authority. The adult child feels the familiar urge to shrink, justify, or placate—but instead, they ground themselves. They respond slowly and calmly, choosing words that reflect boundaries rather than blame: *"I hear what you're saying, and I need to make choices that are right for me now."* Their tone is neutral but firm. They don't argue or explain excessively. They don't lash out. They simply stand in their center, honoring their truth without making the parent the enemy. Over time, this consistency becomes its own gravity. It may not shift the parent's behavior immediately, but it shifts the balance of power in the interaction—making space for the adult child to be sovereign, even in the presence of old dynamics.

Workplace Scenario

An empath enters a corporate meeting where urgency and performative productivity dominate the energy. Though others speak rapidly, compete for airtime, and avoid vulnerability, the empath chooses to speak slowly, asking clarifying questions and naming what's emotionally present in the room. Instead of mirroring the rush, they ground their presence and make space for reflection. Over time, others begin to slow down when they speak, feeling safer in the calm the empath consistently brings. The room's frequency begins to match their clarity—not because they controlled it, but because they held coherence longer than the chaos.

Clarifying Misconceptions: This Is Not Manipulation

Infiltration doesn't mean pretending to be someone you're not. It means choosing which layers of yourself to reveal in real time.

It's how survivors stay alive. It's how prophets move through empires. It's how ancestral truth slips past the gatekeepers of empire and still takes root.

Practice: Map the Layers of You

Create a three-layer map:

Layer 1: The parts of you that are safe and resonant in most environments.

Layer 2: The parts that require trust, timing, and calibration.

Layer 3: The parts that are sacred, rare, and only shared when the soil is fertile. This is your deepest layer.

____

____

____

____

____

____

This map is not about hierarchy—it's about protection and precision.

Presence is not performance. It's calibration.

Strategic presence means:

- Speaking when it counts, not to fill space.
- Withholding when silence is more instructive than speech.
- Entering with coherence rather than urgency.

You don't have to be the most visible to be the most powerful. In fact, those who move with deliberate presence often command more influence than those who are constantly seen.

Real-World Scenarios

- A board member who speaks only once per meeting—but when they do, everyone listens.
- A performer who exits at the peak—not out of fear, but to preserve resonance.

- A teacher who says little in class but changes the entire emotional tone of the room.
- -Oprah Winfrey ended her famous television show at a time that it still had great popularity. Rather than following her usual routine, the last episode was a warm and gracious love letter to her audience. Thus ending the show on a high note—when and how it was right for her.

Practice: Anchor Before Entering

Think about your next high-stakes event or interaction, pause to consider:

- What do you want to transmit?

- What part of me is being asked to show up?

- What part of me needs protection?

____

____

____

____

____

Let this become your ritual of regulation. It's not about how you want to be perceived which can be performative, it's about the mood or tone you want to anchor yourself to.

The Art of Being Without Being Eaten

Visibility is not the goal. Coherence is.
You are not here to contort yourself into digestible pieces for systems that were never built to honor your wholeness.

To be strategic with your presence is not to hide—it is to govern your essence. To reveal only what a space can hold is **not** to withhold truth—it is to protect it from distortion.

Conversely, disrupting a space with your truth may be necessary depending on the scenario. For example, activists throughout history have been known to reveal deep truths to spaces that are not prepared for it, as a means of gaining attention for their cause, while being aware of the potential backlash.

Common examples are sit-ins, banners, and chants at government hearings. Visibility is best when used as a deliberate choice, coupled with strategy. **Ultimately, being decisive and intentional about your presence is key.**

In a world that rewards performance and punishes presence, your task is not to fight for more visibility, but to root more deeply in discernment, timing, and resonance.

Your presence is **not** made powerful by how much of you is seen.

It's made powerful by how much of you remains intact.

Chapter 4

Sacred Disruption – The Design of Interruptions That Heal

4.1 The Precision of Disruption

We've been taught that disruption is loud. That it is reckless, destructive, chaotic.

But sacred disruption is none of these.

It is intentional interruption—not for the sake of noise, but for the sake of clarity. It is how ecosystems rebalance after imbalance.

It is how a body shakes off what it can no longer carry. It is how truth enters when the script has grown too comfortable to question.

Disruption, when wielded with care, is not destruction. It is devotion to something truer.

Insight for Novice Readers

If the idea of sacred disruption feels intimidating, start small.

Disruption doesn't always mean confronting people or calling out injustice publicly. It can be a subtle refusal to participate in what feels false or misaligned. It might mean walking away from gossip, questioning a norm, or simply telling the truth when silence is expected.

Many of us have been conditioned to avoid discomfort at all costs. But discomfort is often where transformation begins. Sacred disruption isn't about making others uncomfortable—it's about refusing to stay small in systems that require your silence.

You don't have to be loud to disrupt. You just have to be aligned. And that alignment often starts with listening to your body—the tension in your shoulders, the breath you hold, the voice that trembles when truth approaches.

Disruption is not a performance. It's a practice of reclaiming presence. And like all practices, it begins one moment, one choice at a time.

4.2 Designing Interruptions That Heal

Sacred disruption is not reactive. It is designed.

While some forms of disruption explode into a space, sacred disruption enters with intention. It is the quiet architect of shift—not shouting in protest, but carving space for presence to rise where suppression once stood. This is not to belittle loud social disruptions, for they too have their place when in it comes to freedom and resistance movements.

To design a meaningful interruption, you must first recognize that most environments follow unspoken scripts. These are the predictable behaviors, tones, and expectations that shape how people interact—whether around a family dinner table, in a workplace meeting, or during a classroom discussion.

Sacred disruptors learn to read those scripts. They notice the emotional patterns, the power dynamics, and the roles everyone plays. Then, instead of reacting impulsively, they wait for the right moment—the moment when truth can be introduced without destroying the space. They don't tear the whole structure down; they shift the energy inside it.

Educational Insight: Timing, Tone, and Threshold

For an interruption to be healing, it must consider three things:

- Timing: Is the space ready—or fractured enough—to receive this truth?
- Tone: Will I speak from self-righteousness or from grounded clarity?

- Threshold: Am I near my emotional edge, or can I stay present through the rupture?

Disruption without discernment can become another form of domination. But disruption with love, precision, and purpose becomes medicine.

Scenario: The Classroom Shift

A Black high school student notices the class consistently skips over the voices of Black authors in the curriculum. One day, instead of lashing out or checking out, they stay after class and say to the teacher: "I've noticed the books we read don't reflect people who look like me. Would you be open to hearing some titles that changed my life?"

This is not about scolding. It's about invitation. And it works—the teacher is more likely to lean in. The syllabus bends. Or when the teacher asks for class commentary, the student can use is as an opportunity to casually mention relevant Black perspectives, writers or histories.

Scenario: Disrupting Narcissistic Patterning

A sensitive adult daughter is on a call with her narcissistic parent, who begins to shift the conversation toward blame: "You never call unless you need something. I guess I don't matter unless I'm useful to you."

Instead of defending herself or absorbing the guilt, she gently says, "I'm not going to continue this conversation while it's centered on blame. If you'd like to talk about how we can connect meaningfully, I'm here for that." Then she pauses. She doesn't argue. She lets silence do the work, even when the silence feels awkward. This is sacred disruption. She doesn't mirror the manipulation. She sets a tone that leaves room for growth—without enabling.

Scenario: Healthcare as a Site of Repatterning

A patient who identifies as nonbinary is repeatedly misgendered during a hospital intake process. Instead of lashing out in frustration, they calmly say to the nurse, "I know these systems weren't built with people like me in mind. But it would mean a lot to be called by the name and pronouns I gave earlier. I'd be happy to clarify again."

The nurse freezes—awkward, embarrassed—but nods. Something in the script just changed. The next time the nurse speaks, they correct themself. This moment may feel small, but it begins a new blueprint within a rigid system. <u>The patient becomes a teacher without taking on the emotional labor of policing</u>.

Insight for Novice Readers

You don't have to be an expert in activism or leadership to design a sacred disruption.

Start by observing patterns. Every space you're in—your home, your workplace, your place of worship—has its own rhythm, its own set of spoken and unspoken rules. Notice when those rules silence you or make others small. Notice what's expected of you that doesn't align with who you really are.

The first step isn't confrontation—it's awareness.

You don't need perfect words. You just need presence. A pause. A question. A breath that slows down what's been moving too fast.

Disruption isn't about control or domination. It's about offering the room a choice: to keep following the old script, or to step into something more truthful.

Every sacred disruptor begins with one moment of courage, spoken in alignment with their deepest truth.

4.3 When Disruption Finds You

Not all disruption is planned. Sometimes, it finds you.

You didn't script the moment. You didn't prepare your voice. But suddenly, you're in the center of a dynamic that demands clarity, boundary, or rupture. These are the moments when the system shows itself—when someone says what no one should say, when silence feels like betrayal, when you feel the full pressure to either conform or disappear.

In these moments, sacred disruption doesn't begin with a plan. It begins with presence.

Educational Insight: Responding Instead of Reacting

When disruption finds you, your first task is not to fix or correct the environment—it's to stay rooted in your body. Most scripts rely on speed, urgency and emotional hijacking. They pull you out of center so quickly that you forget what you know.

The power in these moments comes from your ability to pause. To take a breath. To speak from your alignment rather than your fear.

Responding is not about having the perfect words.
It's about having access to yourself.

Scenario: The Meeting Hijack

During a team meeting, a Black employee shares an idea. Moments later, a white colleague repeats the same idea and receives praise. The moment hangs in the air. Everyone notices—but no one says anything.

The Black employee calmly says, "Thank you for amplifying what I just shared. I'm glad it resonated." The room shifts. The power realigns. This isn't aggression—it's grounded response. A quiet interruption that refuses to let invisibility take root.

Scenario: First Date Boundary

On a first date, a gender-expansive woman finds herself being subtly interrogated by her date: "So... what are you exactly? Like, how do you identify?"

Rather than freeze or perform, she breathes, then smiles gently and says: "I'm not here to make my identity make sense to someone else. I'm here to enjoy honest connection. If that's not where you're coming from, we don't have to continue." She's not dramatic. She's not defensive. She stays centered in her truth—and exits the performance the moment it appears.

Scenario: Interrupting Harm in the Lecture Hall

During a university lecture on global politics, a professor casually refers to African nations as "underdeveloped and culturally stagnant." The room stiffens. No one speaks. A Black student raises their hand— not to argue, but to say, "I'd like to offer a different framing—one that accounts for colonization, resilience, and cultural dynamism. Would you be open to that?"

The professor stumbles. The student remains calm. Their tone is not combative, but firm. The class leans in. A new portal opens.

Scenario: Sacred Silence in the Workplace

In a team meeting where everyone is expected to nod along with a new policy that reinforces unrealistic workloads, one employee chooses not to speak. They don't perform enthusiasm. They don't fake agreement. They simply stay still—eyes steady, breath slow. Their silence isn't passive; it's deliberate. A quiet refusal to participate in the performance.
After the meeting, a colleague whispers, "Thank you. I saw that."

Sometimes, silence interrupts more powerfully than speech. It withdraws silent agreement from the dynamic—without causing disruption or drawing attention.

Insight for Novice Readers:

When disruption finds you, your nervous system may want to flee, freeze, or fawn. That's not failure—it's biology.

Start by recognizing your body's signals. Your clenched jaw, your shallow breath, your racing thoughts—these are invitations to return to your center, not punishments for being unprepared.

You don't need to say something profound in the moment. You only need to stay present long enough to choose a response that honors your integrity.

Sometimes, sacred disruption is as simple as asking a question. Or naming what others pretend not to notice. Or refusing to explain yourself when someone demands it.

Your presence alone—calm, clear, undistorted—is often the most disruptive force in the room.

4.4 Disturbance vs. Disruption

There's a difference between being disturbing and being disruptive.

Disturbance shakes the surface but doesn't shift the system.
It startles, it agitates, it might even go viral. But it doesn't repattern.

Disruption, on the other hand, doesn't just break the silence—it restructures the rhythm.

It doesn't stop at shock or reaction. It listens to the tempo of the room—the unspoken rules, the practiced behaviors—and gently (or firmly) inserts a new beat. Not to destroy, but to retune.

It interrupts the expected and offers a new cadence.
This means it doesn't just name what's wrong—it models another way of being. It introduces a tone that wasn't present before: honesty without attack, clarity without aggression, dignity without apology.

It's not just about being heard—it's about tuning the space to something more coherent.
To be heard is not always enough. Sacred disruption seeks to recalibrate. It aims to restore alignment between what is said and what is real, between what is felt and what is allowed. It is the difference between noise and resonance.

Educational Insight: The Illusion of Impact

In today's performative culture, disturbance is often mistaken for change. A dramatic speech, a viral takedown, a public callout—all these can stir attention. But without coherence, without truth tethered to care, they often dissolve as quickly as they rise.

True disruption happens when presence and precision meet.
It's not performative outrage—it's calibrated influence.

Ask yourself:
• Am I disrupting because I feel centered, or because I feel ignored?
• Is my goal to shift the energy, or to release my own discomfort?
• Will this moment create more clarity—or just more noise?

Scenario to Consider

Subtle Narcissistic Disturbance vs. Grounded Disruption

During a department check-in, a team member known for their charisma and self-focus interrupts others repeatedly, steering the conversation toward their personal grievances. They speak with dramatic flair, name-drop past accomplishments, and position themselves as the overlooked genius. The room becomes tense, then quiet. People nod, but disconnect. Nothing shifts—except the emotional exhaustion in the air.

Later, a quieter colleague raises their hand and says, "I think we're losing sight of the collective work we're here to do. Can we come back to our shared goals and how we're supporting one another?"

Their tone is soft, but steady. The room exhales. The energy recalibrates—not through confrontation, but through coherence.

One person sought attention.
The other restored alignment.

Insight for Novice Readers:

It's easy to mistake attention for transformation—especially in a world where volume is often rewarded more than clarity.

Disturbance might make people look at you. **Disruption** helps them look at themselves.

If you're unsure which one you're practicing, pause and ask: Am I trying to shake the room, or help it hear something deeper? Sacred disruption doesn't always feel dramatic. Often, it feels like restraint, patience, or saying the one thing no one has been able to say.

4.5 The Nervous System as an Instrument of Disruption

Sacred disruption isn't just intellectual—it's physiological.

Your nervous system is the instrument through which you sense dissonance, regulate emotion, and transmit presence. It's not just about what you say or when you act—it's about how your body holds truth in the moment of impact.

People may not remember your exact words. But they'll remember the signal your body gave off—whether it mirrored the chaos, or grounded something deeper.

Educational Insight: Regulation is Strategy

If your system is flooded, your presence becomes reactive.
If your system is grounded, your presence becomes resonant.

Regulation doesn't mean being calm at all costs. It means staying connected to yourself—enough to choose your response, rather than be hijacked by the environment around you.

Disruption is most potent when your tone, breath, posture, and pacing match your deeper knowing. This means your external signals—how you speak, how you move, how you hold yourself—are in harmony with your internal truth. You're not performing confidence. You're not forcing calm. You're simply aligned. That's what makes it powerful.

That coherence is what others feel—even if they can't explain it.

People may not consciously register your words as different—but they feel the steadiness. They notice that your presence doesn't spike, collapse, or demand. Instead, it invites. In a world full of frantic signals, your grounded coherence becomes a kind of signal-jamming—an interruption to noise, and a tuning fork for what is real.

Scenario to Consider

The Scapegoat Who Stopped Playing the Role

During a holiday gathering, a familiar pattern resurfaces. A passive-aggressive comment is made: "Well, if you had your life a little more together like your siblings, we wouldn't have to worry so much."

The room goes quiet. Eyes avert. No one steps in. The scapegoat feels the surge: chest tightens, ears ring, a lifetime of emotional tension suddenly alive again. Their body screams: You're under attack. Defend yourself.

But they don't lash out. They don't fall silent either.

They feel the ground beneath their feet. They inhale—long enough to re-enter their body. And they say, "That kind of comment has followed me for years. I'm not accepting it this time. If we're going to talk, it needs to come from respect."

Their hands shake, but their voice holds. The room shifts. Someone else—usually silent—nods.

Their nervous system was triggered, but instead of fueling collapse or explosion, it became the channel through which the script was broken.

The scapegoat disrupted not just the comment—but the pattern itself.

Practice Tools: Regulating Your System in the Moment

These simple practices can help you stay connected to yourself when your nervous system is activated. Sacred disruption begins with presence.

1. **Feel Your Feet**
Place both feet flat on the ground. Press down gently. Feel the support beneath you. This grounds your energy and signals safety to your body.

2. **Lengthen Your Exhale**
Take a deep breath in through your nose, and exhale slowly through your mouth. Make the exhale longer than the inhale. This helps regulate your vagus nerve and calm your system.

3. **Soften Your Jaw and Hands**
Notice if you're clenching. Consciously release the tension in your jaw, hands, or shoulders. This shifts your body out of defense mode.

4. **Use a Cue Phrase**
Internally repeat a phrase that brings you back to your center. Examples: "I'm safe now." "This moment is mine." "Stay with yourself."

5. **Speak Slower Than You Feel**
When you choose to speak, slow your pace. This keeps you from spiraling into reactivity and models regulation for others.

These are not about bypassing emotions. They are about creating the conditions for your truth to be delivered with power **and** precision.

Insight for Novice Readers

You might think sacred disruption belongs to the brave, the bold, the outspoken. But much of it belongs to the regulated.

This doesn't mean you're always calm. It means you're aware enough to notice when you're triggered—and curious enough to return to yourself instead of collapsing into reaction.

You don't need to be perfect. You don't need to stop feeling. You just need to stay connected—long enough to remember that your body can become a tuning fork for truth.

Your nervous system is not your enemy. It's your compass. The more you listen to it with compassion, the more potent your presence becomes.

Sometimes the most revolutionary thing you can do is pause, feel, and choose.

Remember...

You are the disruption.

Sacred disruption is not about noise—it's about presence. It doesn't demand a spotlight. It holds a signal.

You have the capacity to shift rooms, rewire conversations, and change cultural frequencies—by how you breathe, speak, and show up.

This doesn't require perfection. It requires practice. Practice listening inward before responding outward. Practice grounding yourself before challenging others. Practice trusting that your nervous system, when honored, can become a vessel for profound change.

Whether you whisper or roar, whether you pause or speak, you are already shaping what is possible.

You are not behind. You are not invisible. You are a recalibration in progress.

Your presence, in coherence, is the seed of a more truthful world.

Chapter 5

Narrative Alchemy and the Power of Framing

We are shaped by stories—those told to us, those told about us, and most importantly, those we tell ourselves.

Narrative is not passive. It's architecture.

Narrative builds the walls we walk through. It determines whose voices echo and whose are muted. It tells us what's possible and what is not. Every society is built on a scaffolding of story—often inherited, rarely questioned.

Some of these stories were meant to keep us safe. Others were meant to keep us small.

We carry myths written before we were born: about race, gender, worth, power, ability, love. And unless interrupted, we mistake those myths for truth.

We inherit family roles, societal expectations, and cultural scripts that assign us identities and limitations long before we ever consented.

But narrative is not fixed. It can be bent. Broken. Rewritten.

Narrative alchemy is the sacred work of transforming the story you were given into the story you were meant to live. It is not just about reclaiming your voice—it is about reforging the lens through which reality takes shape.

This chapter is an invitation to remember: you are not the character—you are the author.

You are not the myth—you are the medicine.

When we become conscious of the frames we've been living in, we gain the power to dissolve what distorts—and rewrite what liberates.

5.1 Frames Are Invisible Until You Hit Them

A frame is not just a perspective—it's a boundary of identity and imagination.
It tells you what is "normal," what is "possible," and who you're allowed to be. But most people don't know they're living inside a frame until they try to move beyond it.

Try to dream bigger than what your family believes is "realistic."
Try to dress in a way that contradicts gender norms.
Try to speak truth in a workplace built on hierarchy.
Try to rest in a culture addicted to productivity.

If you've ever felt resistance, ridicule, or withdrawal just for being yourself—you've found a frame.

Frames don't always appear as walls. Sometimes they sound like advice.
Sometimes they look like silence. Sometimes they feel like shame.

These are not just personal obstacles. They are inherited scripts designed to preserve control. And the moment you bump into one— feel the jolt of "You've gone too far"—you are standing at the threshold of narrative alchemy.

The goal isn't to attack the frame.
The goal is to name it, study it, and rewrite the truth it tried to bury.

Educational Insight: How to Identify the Frame You're In

Most frames operate like invisible fences. You don't know they exist until you feel the shock of trying to step outside them.

To begin identifying the frame you're in, ask yourself:

- What parts of me do I have to shrink to feel accepted here?
- What dreams feel dangerous to say out loud?
- When do I feel most performative, most hidden, or most edited?
- Whose approval am I still afraid to lose?

- What fear arises when I open my mouth to speak, and where does that fear come from?

Frames are not just mental—they are physical.
You will often feel them in your body first: a tightening in the chest, a pause in your speech, a discomfort you can't name when entering a particular space.

The body is wise. It remembers the frames others built for us. But it also alerts us to when we are outgrowing them. Your body often knows before your mind does. You may find yourself feeling drained after interactions that once felt normal. You might struggle to tolerate spaces you used to endure. Words catch in your throat not because you're unsure—but because **you know** they'll be misunderstood. You may feel inexplicably angry, sad, or detached when expected to perform a role you've long outgrown. These are not signs of dysfunction. They are signs of expansion. The discomfort is a message: "You don't fit here anymore—not because you're broken, but because you're growing."

To live in coherence, you must begin to see the scripts you've been handed—and then choose which ones are yours to rewrite and which scripts you are meant to walk beyond.

Frames given or imposed onto us are often very rigid. They are designed to hold shape, not to accommodate evolution. Outgrowing a frame often means having to leave—or lovingly distance yourself from—families, old friends, and even jobs that once felt safe or meaningful. Growth, by its nature, will ask you to loosen your grip on the familiar to make room for the true.

Scenarios to Consider

Scenario 1: The Productivity Frame
Narrative: "Your worth is measured by your output."
This frame shows up in workplaces, school systems, and even families. Rest is framed as laziness. Slowing down feels dangerous. You feel guilt when you're not producing something tangible or timestamped.

Nervous System Triggers: Tight chest on weekends. Restlessness during stillness. Anxiety when not "doing."

Narrative Alchemy Begins When: You begin to track your energy instead of your calendar. You ask, "What if being is enough?" You resist urgency with intentional pacing. You take a deep breath as you create moments where you slow down and you give yourself permission to de-prioritize productivity and striving.

Scenario 2: The Respectability Frame
Narrative: "To be taken seriously, you must present yourself like them."
This frame often impacts people of color, queer folks, or anyone from a marginalized identity navigating predominantly white, cisgender, or heteronormative spaces. You edit your voice. You over-explain. You code-switch until you disappear.

Nervous System Triggers: Tension in the throat. Hyper-awareness of posture and tone. Emotional fatigue after socializing.

Narrative Alchemy Begins When: You stop apologizing for your presence. You speak in your own rhythm. You allow your truth to be enough—even if it's not "palatable." You allow yourself to remain silent in your power while others demand your performance.

Scenario 3: The Family Loyalty Frame
Narrative: "Speaking the truth about your upbringing is betrayal."

This frame keeps many people silent about abuse, neglect, or misalignment in family systems. You fear being "disloyal" or "disrespectful." Even in adulthood, you shrink back into the child role.

Nervous System Triggers: Pit in the stomach before family visits. Pressure in the head or temples. Freezing when asked about your past.

Narrative Alchemy Begins When: You choose to be honest. Not to hurt, but to heal. You allow yourself to be loyal to your truth—even when it disrupts the family script.

Scenario 4: The "Freedom" Frame
Narrative: "You are free—and if you're suffering, it's your fault."
This is one of the most enduring American myths. It frames systemic inequity as personal failure. It upholds the illusion of meritocracy while hiding the mechanisms of disenfranchisement. The government says you're free, while limiting access to housing, healthcare, education, and safety. The frame shifts blame downward—onto the poor, the sick, the oppressed.

Nervous System Triggers: Chronic stress about money despite working hard. Shame about asking for help. Exhaustion masked as individual weakness.

Narrative Alchemy Begins When: You name the contradiction. You stop internalizing what was always structural. You ask, "Who benefits from this version of freedom?" You begin to imagine and speak a new frame: liberation that doesn't require perfection, permission, or punishment.

Because when the disenfranchised overwork and stress endlessly about money, those at the top remain unchallenged. Their comfort is subsidized by your exhaustion. Their illusion of stability is built on your forced productivity.

This framing keeps people so tired, so burdened, and so self-blaming that they no longer have the energy or time to organize, protest, or demand better. As worker productivity increases but wages remain stagnant, the wealth gap grows—feeding CEO salaries, corporate profits, and shareholder returns. All while the people creating the value are told they simply aren't working hard enough.

This isn't just economic injustice. It's narrative control.

Practice Exercise: Pause to Reflect

Take a moment to reflect upon a recent family interaction, work setting or any other setting that has had an emotional charge for you.

Consider:

- The underlying narrative that defines the social dynamics and the demands placed on you.
- What emotions and bodily sensations occur in your body.
- How can you practice narrative alchemy within that space?

Describe the narrative frame: The underlying narrative that defines the social dynamics and the demands/expectations placed on you. This is the narrative frame.

____

____

____

____

____

____

What emotions and bodily sensations occurred in your body? These are your nervous system triggers.

____

____

____

____

How can you practice narrative alchemy within this space?

Insight for Novice Readers

Frames are not always easy to spot—especially when you've lived inside them for so long that they feel like truth.

You don't have to dismantle every story overnight. Start by paying attention to when your nervous system tightens, freezes, or wants to run. These are not signs of weakness. They are signals. Clues. Invitations.

Ask yourself: "What version of me is this moment asking for? And what part of me is being left behind?"

When you begin to name the patterns that silence you, shrink you, or guilt you into conformity, you begin to reclaim authorship. And with authorship comes power—not to dominate, but to define.

You are allowed to question the frames. You are allowed to rewrite the script. That questioning is not betrayal. It is awakening.

5.2 Reframing as Power Retrieval

Every story carries a charge.

Some drain you. Some anchor you. Some define you in ways you never consented to—but you live under anyway.

Reframing is the sacred act of removing a story from its original cage and letting it speak in a new voice. It is the act of shining a new light onto an old story.

You may not be able to change what happened, but you can change what it means.

When you reframe a story, you are not erasing your past. You are reclaiming your authorship. You are lifting your experience out of someone else's hierarchy and placing it back in your hands.

This isn't about denial. It's about dignity.

It is the moment you say:
"I am not the failure—I was the one carrying the weight."
"I wasn't too sensitive—I was surrounded by numbness."
"I didn't lose the job—I outgrew the space that couldn't hold my truth."

To reframe is to re-choose yourself—every time someone else tries to write you out of your own life.

Scenarios to Consider

Scenario 1: Reframing a Narcissistic Relationship
At first, they thought the relationship ended because they weren't enough. Too emotional. Too reactive. Too needy.

That's the story they carried. Until they learned about narcissistic dynamics. Until they traced how they had over-functioned, over-explained, and over-gave, all while being slowly erased.

Now, they reframe:

"I wasn't too much—I was in the presence of someone who refused to meet me."

"I didn't fail at love—I learned what it looks like to abandon myself in the name of connection."

This isn't victim-blaming. It's truth reclamation.
The story no longer ends in shame. It ends in sovereignty.

Scenario 2: Reframing Childhood Neglect and Emotional Abuse

For years, they believed they were "too sensitive." That their sadness was a burden. That they were the problem in a family that never had space for their inner life.

But now they see: they were a child responding appropriately to emotional starvation.
They were not defective. They were discerning.

Now, they reframe:
"I wasn't weak—I was attuned."
"My needs weren't wrong—they just didn't fit the story my family needed me to play."

This shift doesn't erase the pain. But it removes the lie.
And that changes everything.

Scenario 3: Reframing a Workplace Confrontation

They were yelled at in a meeting. Loud. Public. Uncalled for.

The executive raised their voice, pointed fingers, questioned their competence in front of others. No one intervened. The room fell silent. Shame flooded their chest. For days, they replayed the moment, wondering what they did wrong—how they could've avoided it.

But with time, they saw the moment for what it was: a performance of dominance.
It wasn't strength—it was fear in disguise.

People who feel truly grounded in their authority don't need to humiliate others to assert it.
Outbursts like these often come from people who feel unstable on the inside.

Instead of responding calmly, they use anger and control as a shield—this hides the fact that they don't know how to manage their emotions, **or** that they feel threatened by being challenged, questioned, or seen too clearly.

What looks like dominance is often just insecurity in a louder costume.

Now, they reframe:

"That outburst wasn't a reflection of my inadequacy—it was a reflection of their insecurity."

"Their volume didn't make them powerful—it made them exposed."

"I wasn't small—I was simply in a room that confused silence with compliance (or weakness)."

The memory still stings, but it no longer defines them.
The frame has shifted. And with it, so has the power.

Practice Tools: Reclaiming Your Story Through Reframing

These exercises are designed to help you gently shift the way you hold past experiences. They don't erase pain—they create space for power.

1. **Name the Old Frame**

Choose a memory that still carries emotional weight. Ask: "What story did I absorb from this experience?" Write it down exactly as it lives in your mind.

2. **Locate the Impact in Your Body**

Close your eyes and recall the moment. Where do you feel it in your body? What sensations arise? Let your nervous system speak before your intellect explains.

3. Identify What Was Missing

What did you need in that moment that you didn't receive? Was it protection? Understanding? Validation? Recognizing this can clarify the emotional truth behind the story.

4. Speak the Reframe Aloud

Use phrases like:
- "Another way to see this is…"
- "Now I understand that I was actually…"
- "That moment didn't mean I was __________; it meant I was __________."

5. **Write a New Ending**

____

____

____

____

____

Journaling

Journal a few sentences from your current self to your past self. What do you want them to know? How can you carry that version of you with more compassion moving forward?

____

____

____

____

____

Reframing is not about spinning a new fantasy. It's about returning to the same story with a new lens—one that honors your truth, your growth, and your inner wisdom.

Insight for Novice Readers

If this feels hard, that's okay. Reframing isn't always instant. It's a process of making meaning from what once made you feel powerless.

You don't need to "get over it." You only need to get closer to the truth that was buried under someone else's story.

Start small. One moment. One sentence. One shift.

Each time you reframe, you're not rewriting the facts—you're reclaiming the frame. And with it, the part of you that never stopped knowing what was real.

Chapter 6

The Power You Didn't Know You Carried

Empaths and the neurodivergent often spend years searching for what's wrong with them. Why they're so sensitive. Why they feel everything. Why rooms exhaust them, why people cling to them, why silence feels louder when they enter. What they rarely ask is this: What if this sensitivity is a type of power—**not** a defect?

Before you learned spiritual language...

Before you had boundaries...

Before you even knew the term empath—you were already tuning the room.

You were the unspoken barometer of truth. You could feel when something was off. You knew when someone's words didn't match their energy. You noticed what others ignored. And without trying, your presence unsettled those hiding behind masks.

That was never weakness. It was frequency.

Empaths carry an inner resonance that functions like a tuning fork. Even in silence, that frequency vibrates into the atmosphere—subtly but unmistakably. Those near you sense the invitation, even if they don't understand it. Some lean in. Others pull away. While others attack. But rarely does anyone remain unaffected.

6.1 The Power You Didn't Know You Were Radiating

You don't have to speak to be felt.

Even in stillness, empaths are tuning forks. The atmosphere shifts when they enter—not because they demand attention, but because they embody coherence. Their nervous system is listening, their heart is awake, and their presence is honest. In a world built on noise, that kind of quiet integrity is jarring. Sometimes even unbearable.

Presence isn't neutral. It carries signal. And for the empath, that signal is often more potent than they realize.

Scenarios to Consider

1. The "Too Much" Employee

An empath enters a new workplace—quiet, respectful, emotionally aware. Within days, a colleague begins to undermine them subtly: interrupting, eye-rolling, or questioning their competence without cause. The empath hasn't spoken up or challenged anyone—but their grounded, sincere presence feels threatening to someone who thrives on chaos, ego-posturing, or groupthink.

Reflection: The hostility is a defense mechanism against feeling exposed or out of control. This is why colleagues like this want to provoke you into expressing the chaos that exists inside them. That's why staying grounded and centered in your own truth prevents you from being swept into their madness.

2. The Uninvited Mirror at a Social Outing

At a party, everyone's drinking heavily, laughing loudly. The empath isn't judging—just sipping water, watching gently, sensing dynamics. Someone gets agitated: "What's your problem?" or "Why aren't you having fun?"

Reflection: The empath's quiet self-possession disturbs those who need constant noise to avoid inner reflection. The empath needn't go into an explanation nor prove that they are having a good time. Simply responding with "I'm enjoying myself in a way that suites me" is a sufficient response.

3. In Friendship

You're sitting across from someone who's always the jokester. But this time, you don't laugh on cue, you don't find it funny. You hold eye contact and deepen your breath. You listen more deeply than they expected. The mood shifts. The jokes taper. Their voice softens. And suddenly they confess something painful they hadn't planned to say. Your attention tuned the room into a space where honesty could emerge.

Reflection: Recognizing when you feel the pull or pressure to perform or act on cue is being self-aware, but that's only the first part. Responding in ways that honor your truth and keeps you grounded is the second, while recognizing the response does not always require words. Your peaceful stillness can be enough.

4. In Family

At a family gathering, one relative is dominating the conversation with subtle jabs and superiority. Others laugh nervously or stay quiet. You don't play along. You don't challenge, either. You redirect the conversation with gentle precision: "Uncle, I hear you, but I'd really love to hear what Auntie thinks about this." The energy shifts. Others follow. Your presence broke the script.

Reflection: These are not loud interventions. They're not displays of dominance. They are frequency realignments. Because even the unhealed empath—the one still discovering their voice, still unsure of their worth—can carry an unmistakable signature of truth. That signature makes them hard to forget.

6.2 Your Light Was Never Passive

Empaths are often told they're "too much" while simultaneously being ignored. This paradox leaves many believing they're invisible—that their kindness goes unnoticed, their softness irrelevant, their presence inconsequential. But this belief couldn't be further from the truth.

Your light was never passive.

It didn't need a microphone or a spotlight to make waves. It disrupted without a word. It softened hard hearts. It revealed what others were trying to hide. Your silence carried weight. Your presence whispered truths too sacred for small talk. And even when no one acknowledged it, it shaped the field.

Even in your unhealed state—before boundaries, before awareness, before language—you were already affecting the energy of rooms. That's why emotionally immature people clung to you. That's why narcissists felt empowered around you. And it's why some people, without even knowing why, tried to dim you.

Because you weren't passive. You were porous. You absorbed what others couldn't name. You felt emotions that weren't yours. You noticed what was never said. Porous doesn't mean weak—it means sensitive to the invisible. Like a sponge in murky water, you took in the unspoken tension, the suppressed grief, the moods others broadcast without realizing. Without training or boundaries, this porousness made you feel like you were the problem. But really, you were just the one attuned enough to feel what the room refused to acknowledge. And in a world addicted to numbness and domination, that made you unforgettable—and, to some, unbearable.

Scenarios to Consider

Scenario 1: The Classroom Ghost Who Was Always Watched

A quiet high school student never raised their hand. They avoided confrontation, kept to themselves. And yet, the teacher would always look at them after a controversial comment, as if silently asking for agreement. Other students whispered that the quiet one gave off "weird vibes." But in truth, the student's energetic integrity was quietly disrupting the group dynamic. Their gaze alone could puncture performance and reveal falseness.

Scenario 2: The "Overlooked" Team Member Everyone Secretly Noticed

A soft-spoken employee never fought for attention. They just did their work with care, helped others without fanfare, and asked powerful questions during tense moments. No one gave them public praise. But when they were out sick, the office felt heavier. Tense. Slightly off. Their absence revealed their influence.

Scenario 3: The Unhealed Friend Who Felt Like a Safe House

You were emotionally messy. Confused. Over-giving. But friends still came to you when they had no one else. They confessed things they couldn't say to anyone. They left your house lighter. You thought you were weak for always listening. But they returned because of your light—even unpolished—was sanctuary.

Clarifying Insight

The world has confused dominance with power, volume with authority, and presence with performance. So when you walked in quietly—attuned, aware, sincere—they didn't have a category for you.

That's why you were underestimated. That's also why you were feared.

You didn't need to perform power. You were power.

And because your power wasn't wrapped in ego or force, it was mistaken for softness—when in fact, it was the foundation others relied on.

Because even the unhealed empath—the one still discovering their voice, still unsure of their worth—can carry an unmistakable signature of truth.

You are not here to vanish into the background. You are not here to carry others' pain as proof of your goodness.

You were not born to dim your light for the comfort of those still hiding in their own shadows.

You, the reader—the unsure sensitive, the slowly healing empath, and even you: the sensitive soul who knows what it's like to carry pain that was never yours—yet it stitched itself into the fabric of your own sorrow. You were never meant to be a shadow holding the shape of someone else's comfort. You were not born to bleed quietly so others could remain loud in their denial.

6.3 You Were Meant to Be Felt

Empaths and sensitive souls are often taught to make themselves smaller, to minimize their needs, to cushion their impact. They are praised for being easygoing, supportive, and selfless—as if these were signs of moral achievement rather than survival strategies.

But you were never meant to shrink.

You were never meant to disappear.

You were meant to be felt.

Even before you knew how to name your truth, people responded to your energy. Your presence called others into deeper reflection. Your kindness disarmed defenses. Your disappointment pierced deeper than raised voices. You didn't have to demand attention. You simply walked in, and the air changed.

You were not here to absorb pain as proof of love. You are not a sponge for other people's wounds. You are a mirror, a tuning fork, a threshold. You are what the nervous system recognizes before the mind can explain.

You're not here to prove your strength by fighting.

You're here to show that your energy is too sacred to waste. Your time, too precious to squander.

The world will tell you that this is selfish. That putting yourself first is wrong. That being seen, heard, and honored must be earned.

But they are wrong.

You are not here to vanish into the background.

You are not here to carry others' pain as proof of your goodness.

You are not here to heal everyone—only to stand in your frequency long enough for others to remember theirs.

You're the one who can change the temperature of a room without speaking.

You're the one whose absence says more than others' presence.

You're the one who can make silence safe again.

This is not an accident.

This is your design.

You were meant to be felt.

6.4 The Mirror That Exposes What They Can't Admit

Empaths often wonder, *"Why did they lash out at me? I didn't do anything."*

And that's exactly the point.

You didn't attack.

You didn't accuse.

You didn't posture.

You simply *were*—and that was enough to unmask what they'd spent years hiding.

Because your presence is a mirror. Not the kind you hang on a wall, but the kind that reflects the invisible. Your energy, your sincerity, your attunement to what's unspoken—these qualities don't just comfort others. They reveal and expose others. And not everyone is ready to be seen.

Even in your unhealed state, you noticed contradictions. You felt emotional currents no one named. You could sense a lie—even if it wore a smile. And without saying a word, your field made others squirm.

Not because you were wrong, but because they couldn't bear to face what your presence revealed in them.

Your very existence threatened the denial they needed to survive.

You didn't need to expose them.

You *reminded* them...

Of what they gave up to fit in.

Of what they silenced to feel safe.

Of what they lost in the pursuit of control, status, or validation.

And when someone isn't ready to face those truths, they often blame the mirror. They call you "too intense," "too sensitive," "too emotional." But what they really mean is: *You make me feel things I've buried too deep... Your presence awakens the skeletons I've hidden in my closet.*

Your presence becomes disruptive—*not because you're chaotic,* but because you don't match the performance everyone else agreed to.

Your gaze becomes unsettling—*not because you're judgmental,* but because you see through masks they forgot they were wearing.

Your silence becomes loud—*not because you're passive-aggressive,* but because it echoes in the hollowness of their own avoidance.

Empaths don't just hold space.

They *illuminate* it.

And in doing so, they awaken discomfort in those who have built their identities on suppression.

Let's be clear:

This is not your fault.

This is your power.

6.5 The Cost of Being Misunderstood

Empaths often walk through life carrying a question they can't quite name:

"Why does my presence feel like too much and not enough at the same time?"

You speak softly and they call you avoidant.

You speak boldly and they call you intense.

You set boundaries and they say you're cold.

You extend compassion and they say you're naïve.

This is the cost of being attuned in a world that confuses sensitivity with fragility, and authenticity with danger.

You are not misunderstood because you're unclear.

You're misunderstood because most people have never met someone who doesn't hide behind a mask.

The world has no language for unfabricated presence.

So instead, they translate your essence through the only vocabulary they know: performance, power-plays, and personas.

But you were never fluent in such games.

What you offer isn't performative—it's vibrational.

And that terrifies people who've never slowed down long enough to hear the truth echoing in silence.

Real-World Scenarios

In the workplace: You say no to taking on extra work without compensation. A colleague whispers that you're "entitled" or "difficult." They don't see the years you've said yes out of guilt or fear. They only feel the shift in your energy—and mistake your self-respect for arrogance.

In relationships: You ask for emotional presence instead of surface-level affection. Instead of meeting you there, they accuse you of being "too demanding" or "never satisfied." But really, they're being asked to meet a depth they've never practiced.

In your family: You stop playing the role that made others comfortable. The peacemaker. The caretaker. The quiet one. Suddenly, you're told you've changed. That you're "not the same." And they're right—you've stopped shrinking.

Educational Insight: Misinterpretation as Projection

People don't always see you as you are.

They see you as they feel around you.

And when someone feels exposed, inferior, or emotionally unstable in your presence, they often interpret that discomfort as your fault.

They don't realize your presence simply illuminated what they were avoiding.

They call you "too much" because you reflect the places in them that feel not enough.

They call you "manipulative" because they can't track your power.

They call you "strange" because you don't play by rules they never questioned.

But none of these labels are yours to hold.

For the Novice Reader

If you're just beginning to notice this pattern—pause before internalizing the judgments others place on you.

Ask yourself:

Is this feedback rooted in love, or in discomfort?

Am I truly unclear—or are they unready to see me clearly?

What parts of myself am I shrinking to stay legible to others?

Being misunderstood doesn't mean you've failed to express yourself.

Sometimes, it means you've outgrown the script others wrote for you.

Practice Tool: Sensing the Impact of Your Presence

Try this exercise the next time you enter a room or social setting:

1. Before Entering

Pause for a moment and breathe deeply.

Say silently: "I am not here to fix, prove or make someone feel less guilty. I am here to be present in my full truth."

2. While in the Room

Notice how people respond to your silence or your gaze

Observe the atmosphere without trying to change it.

Stay grounded in your body—feel your feet, your spine, your breath.

3. After You Leave

Reflect: What shifted in the room, if anything?

Did someone become more vulnerable? More performative? More reactive?

What did you feel in your body, and what might that tell you?

This tool isn't about ego or control. It's about becoming aware of how your energetic coherence creates resonance, discomfort, or invitation. Over time, you'll learn to read this feedback without taking it personally.

6.6 You Were Never Too Much

There comes a point in every empath's path when the question shifts from "How can I be more palatable?" to "Why am I shrinking in the first place?"

This is not a question of manners. It is a question of sovereignty.

You have been asked to dim. To soften your truth. To compress your instincts. Not because you were wrong—but because your full presence disrupted a room addicted to suppression.

So you learned to second-guess your intuition.

You apologized for your boundaries.

You laughed off the moments you should have cried through.

But here's the truth: **You were never too much.**

You were too *honest* for dishonesty to breathe easily.

Too *awake* for people committed to sleepwalking.

Too *whole* for systems built on fragmentation.

Even in your doubt, you tuned the frequency of rooms. Even in your confusion, you raised the standard for presence. Even when you didn't know your worth, you radiated it.

This section is your invitation to stop editing your existence.

Breathe deeper. Speak fuller.

Occupy the full range of who you are.

Because the people who told you to "calm down" were often the ones who needed your calm to keep their chaos unexamined.

Your presence is not a disruption. It's a recalibration.

You were never "too much."

You were *more than they were ready to face.*

6.7 The Gravity of Self-Recognition

You've spent years absorbing, attuning, and adapting to others' needs. Your nervous system became fluent in scanning for danger, for discomfort, for disapproval. But there comes a moment—subtle but seismic—when you turn that exquisite sensitivity inward.

The gaze that once searched others now returns home.

Self-recognition is not narcissism. It's not ego. It's the moment you realize: *I am not broken. I am broadcasting.*

You are not a sponge. You are a signal tower.

You are not meant to *only* mirror. You are meant to radiate.

And when you recognize your own frequency—your tone, your rhythm, your emotional signature—you begin to shape how others meet you. Not because you demanded it. But because you remembered yourself first.

Your nervous system, once hijacked by external validation, begins to attune to your own pace. Your own knowing. Your own needs. This shift doesn't scream. It hums. And that hum builds gravity.

People notice. They soften. Or they resist. But they cannot ignore.

This is what happens when you stop over-explaining. When you stop apologizing for your emotions. When you speak with your full voice— not to convince, but to *reveal*.

You become a frequency—clearer than before, more stable than before. And others calibrate around you.

This is not domination. This is not manipulation.

This is *coherence*.

Scenario to Consider

The Rising Pulse of Self-Return

A mid-career professional, long known for being agreeable and emotionally attuned to their team, begins to feel the weight of constant accommodation. They've always been the peacemaker— the one others vent to, rely on, lean into for emotional stability. But internally, they're exhausted.

One day, during a high-pressure meeting, someone tries to interrupt them—again. But this time, the empath doesn't shrink. They pause, breathe, and with steady calm, say: "I'd like to finish my thought."

The room stills. It's not the words—it's the presence. The shift is apparent. The new clarity is palpable. They continue speaking—not to dominate, but to be *in* the room, not *beneath* it.

Later, a colleague says, "You felt different today. More... solid."

That's the moment of gravity. Not louder. Not harsher. Just more tuned to *self* than to the performative chaos around them. And the whole dynamic begins to bend—not because they demanded power, but because they embodied it.

6.8 Your Frequency Is the Friction

You've been told you're "too sensitive," "too intense," or "too much." But here's what was never said:

Your frequency is what they couldn't metabolize.

You weren't being *too much*—you were vibrating in truth. And truth creates friction in systems built on pretense. You didn't argue, perform, or rebel. You just *were*. And that was enough to make egos flinch, lies tremble, and illusions start to crack.

In a world conditioned to reward performance, suppression, and conformity, your presence was a signal flare. Not because you were loud—but because your energy refused to collapse into compliance. You became friction to systems that needed your silence to function.

People don't always hate you because you're wrong.

Sometimes they resist you because you're right—and your **resonance exposes what they're not ready to face**.

Real-World Scenario

The Empath in the System

You work in an office where gossip is currency, burnout is pride, and self-neglect is rewarded. You don't play along. You don't gossip. You protect your rest. You work with care, not urgency.

Soon, people start calling you "distant," "not a team player," or "aloof."

But deep down, they know you're holding a standard that reflects what they gave up long ago: integrity, balance, and inner stillness.

You became friction—not by pushing, but by standing.

Clarifying Insight

You are not misunderstood because you're broken. You are resisted because you're different.

Your presence reminds others of their disconnection—from themselves, from truth, from soul.

And when they're not ready to return to themselves, they turn away from you—or lash out.

Friction isn't failure. It's confirmation.

Exercise: Discern the Friction

Think about a recent intense moment and then ask yourself:

Did I experience resistance because I was out of alignment? *Or because I was in deeper alignment than this space allowed? Why*

____

____

____

____

____

____

____

Was the discomfort asking me to shrink—or to root deeper into my center?

How can I let this friction affirm that I'm no longer collapsing to keep the peace?

By reaching this point, you've done something many never pause long enough to do: you've turned toward your own perception with curiosity instead of judgment. You've begun to see the patterns beneath the patterns, the structures beneath the stories, and the ways power moves—both around you and within you.

As you close this book, remember this: the insights you've encountered here are not meant to be applied once and perfected. They are meant to *return to you*, again and again, as life presents new situations, relationships, and thresholds.

There will be moments when clarity arrives only after the fact—when you recognize a power dynamic in hindsight or see, with new understanding, how you might respond differently now. This is not a failure. It is how integration works. Awareness often comes first as recognition, then as embodiment.

Be gentle with yourself when understanding comes late. It doesn't mean you missed something—it means your perception is deepening.

This guide was never meant to make you flawless. It was meant to make you *practiced*.

Life will continue to offer opportunities to honor yourself—sometimes quietly, sometimes imperfectly, sometimes with more grace than you expected. Each moment becomes a place to experiment with coherence, boundaries, language, and rhythm. Over time, returning to your center will feel less effortful and more instinctive.

Do not seek perfection. Seek practice.

There may always be room for refinement—and that is not a flaw. It is evidence that you are alive, responsive, and still in relationship with your power.

You do not have to walk this path alone.

I offer both **one-on-one and group coaching** rooted in the concepts and practices found in this book, for those who want guidance, reflection, and support as they continue this work in real time.

You can reach me directly at **BrittonSpeaks@gmail.com** — please include the word **"Flamekeeper"** in the subject line so I know you're writing from this space.

You can also connect with me on social media at **@BrittonSpeaks** (my handle is the same across all platforms). For the most up-to-date offerings, resources, and ways to work together, follow the link in my social media bio.

Return to these pages whenever something feels unclear. Let new experiences illuminate familiar words. What resonates now may deepen later.

You are not behind. You are becoming fluent.

The remembering continues—each time you choose coherence over compliance, self-trust over self-erasure, and presence over performance.

And that choice, made again and again, is the practice.

Author's Additional Works

Wonder: A New Testament is a lyrically poetic, genre-blending collection of short stories that merges memoir with myth, fantasy with philosophy. Through spiritual allegory, ancestral folklore, and imaginative storytelling, Britton Lee explores love, identity, loss, and creation— inviting readers to see the world with renewed curiosity and tenderness.

Featuring prophetic starfish, talking stones, and nature as a guiding presence, *Wonder* offers new language for expressing love and meaning. Each piece gently causes the reader to pause, reflect, and remember the quiet knowing we often forget we carry.

Intimate yet expansive, *Wonder: A New Testament* is an invitation to feel deeply, think differently, and return to a sense of awe.

ISBN:

Paperback 979-8-218-51553-9

Hardcover 979-8-218-53221-5

E-book 979-8-218-52432-6

Britton Lee, MPH

NOTES & REFLECTIONS

NOTES & REFLECTIONS

NOTES & REFLECTIONS

Britton Lee, MPH

NOTES & REFLECTIONS

NOTES & REFLECTIONS

Britton Lee, MPH

NOTES & REFLECTIONS

NOTES & REFLECTIONS

145

NOTES & REFLECTIONS

NOTES & REFLECTIONS

147

NOTES & REFLECTIONS